Smart Skills: Meetings

Smart Skills: Meetings

Patrick Forsyth

Independent Book Publisher

Legend Business, 107-111 Fleet Street
London EC4A 2AB
info@legend-paperbooks.co.uk
www.legendpress.co.uk

Contents © Patrick Forsyth 2019

The right of Patrick Forsyth to be identified as the author of
this work has been asserted by him in accordance with the
Copyright, Designs and Patent Act 1988.

British Library Cataloguing in Publication Data available.

ISBN 978-1-78955-0-320
Set in Times

Cover designed by:
Linnet Mattey | www.linnetmattey.com

CONTENTS

Foreword

Myriads of management handbooks in print purport to provide guidance on the key skills to success and business training manuals also abound. Generally, they suffer from one or both of two defects.

Sometimes, the scope of the book is too broad. Attempting to provide comprehensive advice on all the basic business activities, there is no clear message. Nobody can gain proficiency in every field of marketing and sales, administration, purchasing, bookkeeping and financial management in a short period of time, although those who start their own businesses do need to acquire a working knowledge of most. Other titles fail to distinguish between technical capability and personal skills.

However, there are a handful of personal and interpersonal skills that are essential ingredients for success in any business: the private or public sectors and the professions; large or small organisations; employees, business owners or management consultants. These are the subject matter of the Smart Skills series on which all readers can focus to advantage because mastery of them will surely enhance both job satisfaction and their careers.

Patrick Forsyth, series editor and author of this first title, "Meetings" is a well known writer of down-to-earth management training guides. Skill in convening and participating in meetings, leading discussions in order to arrive at constructive decisions, and managing the fall-out and follow-up from meetings is fundamental to establishing yourself as a respected and effective member of the community in which you work. This topic provides a logical starting-point for the series.

In the Smart Skills series Patrick and his fellow authors bring together their know-how of core skills into a single compact series.

Whatever your level of experience and the rung of your career ladder that you have reached, this book will help you to audit your personal effectiveness and raise your game when interacting with others.

Jonathan Reuvid

INTRODUCTION

The agenda for success

The ideal meeting is two with one absent
Traditional saying

Meetings are ubiquitous. Yet many people spend so much time in them, and so many of them somehow end up being unconstructive, to say the least. Just saying the word 'meeting' is sufficient in some organisations for people to conjure up a picture of the typical smoke-filled room of old, a table covered with papers – and that covered, in turn, with the rings from coffee cups – and of wasted time, boredom, acrimony, delay, argument, frustration and decisions not made. How often have you come out of a meeting and not only felt dissatisfied but wondered what you had been doing there at all? If you answer that you never feel like that, then you must work for a truly exceptional organisation; and I'm not sure that many people would find it very easy to believe you. For many it is a regular feeling.

So, meetings can be hard work, difficult, boring and too often end up serving no useful purpose and advancing things or prompting decisions not at all. But meetings are, however, necessary to communication – with colleagues, bosses, subordinates, customers, whoever – and they must be made to work and work well. The old saying quoted at the top of the page was perhaps coined because such an approach ensures action really does follow. Meetings are the archetypal mixed blessing. They are time consuming and thus incur costs and not just in money terms. The dangers are all too obvious and include meetings that:

- Waste time.
- Waste money, directly or indirectly.
- Divert attention from more important tasks.
- Slow down progress and delay action.
- Are divisive.
- Lower morale.
- Are a platform for the talkative and disruptive.
- Breed office politics.
- Create muddle and chaos.

You could doubtless add to that list. Such meetings end up prompting few (or bad) decisions, or simply end in tears. There is also a different sort of cost involved here – the opportunity cost. In other words, think about what else could be being done – *achieved* – if people were not in a meeting, and consider how much those other activities might be worth. Additionally, in an organisation of any size the negative effects of an unconstructive meeting can be multiplied by the number of people involved. That thought is scary. So never say, "It's just a meeting"; never overlook the costs; instead you should aim to make sure meetings are always productive and useful.

Meetings *are* in fact an important part of communications inside and outside the organisation in terms of consultation, debate and decision-making. We do need them; or at least we need some of them. Hence this publication: there are principles and techniques involved. This is no lost cause. It is an area where some consideration and, perhaps, also some discipline and cultivation of the right habits works wonders. Meetings not only *can* be constructive, they *have* to be. Time is too valuable a resource for us to allow any of it to be frittered away on ineffective meetings. Most organisations have plenty of other things that need to be done – and important things at that.

So, we must get the most from them; and we do not need them to be too numerous, too long or, above all, unconstructive. What is more, good, effective meetings do not just happen. No deep law of meetings means we must put up with bad ones in order to get an occasional good one thrown in, and a culture of effective meetings will not exist unless everyone in an organisation actively works at creating and maintaining it. Everybody's role is important, whether running a meeting or attending one.

THE BEST OF MEETINGS

Whatever the meeting, large or small, formal or informal, long or short, if it is planned, considered and conducted specifically to make it go well, then it can be made effective – whatever its purpose. Meetings can seek to do numbers of things. They can be used to:

- Inform.
- Analyse and solve problems.
- Discuss and exchange views.
- Inspire and motivate.
- Counsel and reconcile conflict.
- Obtain opinion and feedback.
- Persuade and perhaps impress.
- Progress projects.
- Train and develop.
- Reinforce the status quo.
- Prompt change in knowledge, skills, or attitudes.

And more; you can no doubt add to this list too. Remember also that such intentions are not mutually exclusive. A particular meeting may be aiming to do a number of things together. With the key purpose of most meetings often being to prompt change, then to do that means making decisions (there is surely no point in having a meeting if everything is going to remain the same). So any meeting must be constructive: putting people in a position where *good* decisions can prompt *appropriate* action.

Additionally, good meetings are not just useful: they can stimulate creative discussion and action that would never occur unless a particular group got together. As has been said, we all need some meetings and their role and importance can vary. They may simply be a form of communication, but good meetings are not just useful: most people positively *want* meetings. Having too few can be as big a mistake as having too many. Why do people want them? There are various reasons, but people believe that meetings can, for example:

- Keep them informed and up-to-date.
- Provide individuals with a chance to be both seen and heard.

- Create involvement with others.
- Be useful social gatherings.
- Allow cross-functional contact.
- Provide individuals with public relations opportunities.
- Can broaden experience and prompt learning.

And they are right. Meetings *are* potentially useful. Indeed the progress of an organisation can, in a sense, be made certain only if meetings are held and go well.

First base

For a meeting to be truly successful, ensuring its success cannot begin only as the meeting starts – the "I think we're all here, what shall we deal with first?" school of meeting organisation. Making it work starts before the meeting, sometimes some time before.

First, ask some basic questions, for example: is a meeting really necessary? Should it be a regular meeting? (Think very carefully about this one; once a meeting is designated as the weekly, monthly or whatever, XYZ meeting it can become a routine that is difficult to break and, as such, can be an especially easy way to waste time.) Who should attend? (And who should not?)

If you are clear in these respects then you can proceed. Some key points to bear in mind include:

- *Setting an agenda:* this is very important; no meeting will go well if you simply make up the content as you get under way (notify people of the agenda in advance and give good notice of contributions required from others).
- *Timing:* set a meeting start time and a finishing time, then you can judge its conduct alongside the duration and even put some rough timing to individual items to be dealt with. Respect the timing too: always start on time and try to stick with the duration planned.
- *Objective:* always set a clear objective – in advance – so that you can state clearly *why* a meeting is being held (and the answer should never be – *because it is a month since the last one!*). See box.

12

The following classic tale makes a good point about objectives for a meeting needing to be clear *in advance*:

A medieval King is crossing the forest with his entourage on a hunting trip. On a series of trees they see a painted target and in the exact centre of each there is an arrow. "What incredible accuracy," says the King, "We must find the archer."

Further on they catch up with a small boy carrying a bow and arrow. He is frightened at being stopped by the King's party, but admits that he fired the arrows. "You did shoot the arrows, didn't you?" queried the King, "You didn't just stick them into the targets by hand?" The boy replied, "Your majesty, I swear I shot all the arrows from a hundred paces." "Incredible," said the King, "You must accept a job at the palace, I must have an archer of such brilliance near me. But tell me, you are so young, how do you achieve such accuracy?"

The boy looked sheepish. "Well," he said, "first I step out a hundred paces, then I fire the arrow into the tree... and then I walk back and paint the target on the tree."

This is perhaps the equivalent of the corporate habit of only deciding what a meeting is about after it has started.

- *Prepare yourself:* read all necessary papers, check all necessary details and think about how you will handle both your own contribution and the stimulation, and control, of others.
- *Insist others prepare also:* this may mean instilling habits (if you pause to go through something that should have been studied before the meeting then preparation is immediately seen as not really necessary).
- *People:* consider what roles individuals attending should have: making a case, reporting back, observing and more.
- *Environment:* a meeting will work best if people attending are comfortable: so organise for no interruptions and switch the coffee pot on and the phones off.

Then, at the appointed hour, someone must take charge and make the meeting go well.

In many organisations meetings are unproductive or unconstructive not because how they are undertaken is ill-considered, but rather because making them successful is hardly considered at all. There is a real opportunity here (one worth convening a meeting to discuss?).

Enough scene-setting. Let us turn now to how to make meetings work, and investigate these issues and more in some detail. All good meetings need an agenda (the contents page contains the equivalent here).

Ahead of any meeting any relevant matters that can help make it go well need to be considered, and specifically you need to think about:

1. How the leadership – the so-called Chair* of a meeting can make a valuable contribution.
2. How to be a (successful) participant (although there are lessons here for chair people too and for participants in number one).
3. The overall dynamics and interactions within meetings and the different kinds of communication involved.
4. And last, but not least, what should happen after the meeting.

So, what should we consider before a meeting even begins? The next chapter investigates.

* Note: In the past, the person conducting a meeting was always traditionally referred to as the Chairman, regardless of the gender of the incumbent. In more politically correct times, the term used more commonly became Chair or Chairperson. Recently, some women acting in this capacity seem again happy to be called Chairman. Here, the term Chair or Chairperson are both used, though what matters, of course, is the role and not the title given to it.

Chapter 1

BEFORE MEETINGS START:
setting them up for success

**Meetings are indispensable when you don't
want to do anything**
JK Galbraith

If a meeting is to be truly successful then its purpose and content have
to be thought through first. The "I think we're all here, what shall we
deal with first?" school of meeting conduct already referred to is
unlikely to lead to success. Making meetings work starts before the
meeting does – sometimes long before.

IS YOUR MEETING REALLY NECESSARY?
There may be other ways of dealing with the business in hand. So the
first question is whether a meeting needs to be called or, if it is not your
meeting, needs to be attended. Consider yours first.

Your meetings
The first thing, as with so much in office life, is to ask questions. Never
just open your mouth and say, "We had better schedule a meeting."
Pause and think. Ask yourself: is it a matter for debate or consultation?
Or can a decision be made without either of those? Can any information
that will be disseminated at the meeting be circulated in any other way?
If a brief conversation is all that is necessary, might it not be enough to

have a word on the telephone, in the corridor, or over a working lunch?

Note: Although conference calls have an awkwardness (because they are voice only) the technology is improving all the time, including systems based on video and they are increasingly providing a viable option in some situations, especially when people are geographically spread. As soon as you ask such questions, an alternative can often present itself, and that may well be one less time-consuming than a meeting.

Remember that such decisions affect not only your own time. Six people meeting for an hour represent six hours' work time (plus preparing, getting there and... but you get the point); and this is the way to think about it. Of course, the more people you invite to a meeting the more this situation multiplies; and large meetings tend, by their very nature, to last longer than smaller ones.

Other people's meetings

What about meetings called by others? Although there will always be some you have to attend, the principle of "think first" still applies. You may find there are some meetings that you attend for the wrong reasons. For example, it is very easy to find you are really going only to keep in touch or "just in case something important crops up". If that is the case, then maybe it will be sufficient just to read the minutes or check with someone who did attend for a two-minute update. Even if, for those that manage other people, you feel it is important for your department to be represented you can always delegate someone else to attend and report back to you.

There may be aspects of a forthcoming meeting that you would enjoy or find interesting, topics on which your contribution would allow you to shine, but still it may not be a priority to attend. There is an old story, which perhaps illustrates the attitude to take, about a training manger who scheduled a workshop on delegation skills and sent round a note indicating that certain managers were expected to attend. One promptly replied he would not do so ... but that he would send his assistant!

In any case, whatever the meeting is about, make sure it is essential, that your presence is useful and that there is no alternative to meeting;

and then read the rest of this chapter before you finalise matters and the meeting gets underway!

Regular meetings

If it is important to consider whether any one meeting is necessary then it is doubly important to consider carefully before getting locked into a series of regular meetings. There are all too many weekly or monthly meetings that continue to be held for no better reason than because they have become a habit. If this is the case, then few of them are likely to be useful. Indeed, I would go so far as to suggest banning labelling any meeting in a way that is prefixed by a word such as "weekly"; certainly think long and hard before you allow such a tag to be brought into use.

Admittedly, meetings scheduled in advance are usually important. Often it also makes sense to have them on a regular or semi-regular basis. But it may be better to think in terms of, say, ten a year rather than one a month: regularity may be varied to match such things as the seasonal pattern in a business (or just the calendar year), with meetings being set closer or further apart at certain times of the year. Get over the problem of gathering busy people together by scheduling ahead by all means, but be warned: this is an area from which stem many unproductive meetings and much waste of time.

One of a regular series of meetings can always be cancelled, of course, although I have often heard managers say something like "Let's let it stand and see what people have to say". In this (probably well intentioned) way a manager can easily earn a reputation for running useless meetings. It is an area where a more ruthless attitude really is likely to be best.

But if a meeting is to happen, what will make it effective?

THE AGENDA

Every meeting needs an agenda. In most cases this needs to be in writing and be circulated to everyone involved in advance (and that doesn't mean ten minutes before the start time!). This is surely basic, though in practice it is often not done. A clear agenda can shape and control a meeting in all sorts of ways. It is ultimately the responsibility of the Chair to compile the agenda, though others may have a role in this too. Not least it should:

- Specify the formalities (do you need to note any apologies for absence, for example?).
- Pick up and link points from any previous meetings to ensure continuity.
- Help individuals to prepare themselves.
- Give people an opportunity to make additional agenda suggestions (something made possible by advance circulation).
- Specify who will lead or contribute to each item.
- Order the items for discussion to review; this is something that may need to represent the logical order of the topics, the difficulty they pose (and perhaps the time they occupy), and the participants' convenience (maybe someone must leave early and you want something dealt with before this happens).
- Reflect any "hidden" agendas, for example with a controversial issue being placed to minimise discussion (just before lunch, say); or indeed to just avoid this sort of thing happening
- Deal with administrative matters such as where and when the meeting will be held and, if it is going to be lengthy, when any breaks or refreshments will come.

Sequence is also important. Selecting a good order in which to go through things can make all the difference. For example, is a particular item:

- Best addressed early on, to get it out of the way while people are fresh?
- Best placed to provide a link with other items (horses first, carts second)?
- The most dependent on preparation?
- Interesting or important to everyone attending, or to just a few?
- In danger of taking too much time and overshadowing other things, or does it have any characteristics – being awkward, unpopular, contentious, or easy, straightforward, quick – that makes it suit a particular placing?

Furthermore, any agenda must be realistic, so whoever is organizing it should ask themselves the following questions:

- Will all the items on the agenda fit within the time available?
- Is there sufficient lead time before it is scheduled for notification and preparation?
- Will one major item put time and attention for the rest of the meeting in jeopardy?
- Are items matched to participants? (Are the right people going to be there – or not?)
- Is the style of the meeting right? (Training or persuasion may take longer than information giving, for example).

It is too late to do anything about it if you find out only after your meeting is underway that the way it was set up is preventing it from operating effectively.

The overall look and balance of an agenda should be checked to make sure that the meeting is not attempting too much in the time available. If patience runs out things will end up taking longer, or will not have justice done to them. Above all, the agenda should reflect the objectives of the meeting. (Indeed, a fully stated agenda may sometimes address why something is being tabled as well as the plain fact that it is). Before going any further, therefore, we turn to objectives.

Why are we meeting?

Sometimes meetings do not become ineffective because of how they proceed: rather they are doomed from the start because they do not have clear, specific objectives. You must not meet in order to:

- Start the planning process.
- Discuss cost savings.
- Review training needs.
- Improve administration.

Set clear, explicit objectives, what are often referred to as SMART – see box). Avoid vaguely worded items such as "discuss reducing expenditure"; say instead that you want "to decide how to reduce the advertising budget by 10 percent over the next six month". If clear objectives are set it will help in a number of ways:

- People will understand why the meeting is taking place.

- They will be better able, and perhaps more inclined, to prepare.
- The discussion will be more focused.
- The proceedings will be easier to control.

The net result is that the meeting is more likely to achieve its aims.

Making objectives useful
Objectives should be SMART. This well-known mnemonic stands for specific, measurable, achievable, realistic and timed, thus any objectives should be:

Specific – expressed clearly and precisely.

Measurable – it must be possible to tell later if you have achieved something (the difference between saying costs should "be reviewed" and "costs must be reduced by 10% by the end of the financial year").

Achievable – objectives must not be so difficult as to be pie in the sky; otherwise the plan that goes with them similarly becomes invalid and of no practical help in taking things forward.

Realistic – it must fit with the broad picture and be what you want; it might be a valid objective to aim for something possible but not ideal (maybe those costs can be reduced by axing something) but this will not be helpful (if, say, customer service levels and thus revenue declines). Action is needed with more ambitious objectives in mind.

Timed – this is important; objectives are not to be achieved "eventually" but by a particular moment: when do you aim for something to be done, this year, next year or when?

Time and timing
In a busy world time is always of the essence; here we deal with several aspects of it with regard to meetings.

Starting time
Basics first: every meeting needs a starting time. Exactly when that is can affect what happens subsequently. Do you want a meeting that lasts just an hour? If so, then 12 noon or 4pm are good times: the meeting will not drag on if people want to get to lunch or go home. Equally a

meeting at 8:30am may give you an uninterrupted hour before most of the distractions of the day start to crowd in. Choose your time well, in context of how the organisation and the group of people operate, and stick to it. This may sound simple, but it needs some thought and resolve.

Respect for time

This is fundamentally important. Nothing is guaranteed to get a meeting off to a worse start, with everyone in a bad mood, than the consequences of poor timekeeping. Imagine the scene: people congregate, it is time to start the meeting, but not everyone is present. It is decided to "give them five minutes". Coffee is poured. Various ad-hoc (and probably not very useful) discussions start. Time passes and finally the meeting starts 15 minutes late with one person still to arrive. Ten minutes later, just as things are getting down to business, the latecomer arrives. Apologies and bringing the latecomer up-to-date waste another five minutes, and so on, and so on... and, of course, the greater the number of people attending the meeting, the greater the waste and irritation.

So always start meetings on time. It is worth repeating: always start meetings on time.

Doing so may be difficult at first, but the only way to crack the problem is to instill habits and respect. An early boss of mine once literally locked me out of a meeting and explained later that he had done it to make a point; he had – and I was never late for a meeting with him again.

If someone is late, say so! Try not to recap unless it's vital; it just wastes more time for everyone who was punctual (do it one-to-one at the end, perhaps). Be consistent. Let the word go round: "You'd better not be late for one of Patrick's meetings!" It is really worth the effort. Human nature being what it is, you will not succeed 100 per cent with everyone, but this is no reason to give up and admit defeat. It is worth persisting, because the attitudes struck here are highly beneficial – and, perhaps, to more than simply the efficiency of a meeting; good time management and concentration on priorities is important for everyone in an organisation.

Finishing time

Every meeting should have not only a starting time but also a finishing time. It is a courtesy to people (and helps keep the meeting on track) to set aside a specific time for a session. As well as helping the meeting, this also helps people plan and allocate their use of time after the meeting. So, although you can always finish early, you should try not to overrun. The more you do this the better you will get at judging how much time things are likely to take.

A timed agenda

Similarly, it helps to have items on the agenda timed (perhaps not every last one, but certainly the main topics). Again this helps focus discussion and will give you something to aim for – "Let's try to sort this out in the next 15 minutes". It really does help.

Note: it is good practice to check your diary when you must schedule a meeting; not simply to see if you can attend at the stated time, but to see how doing so may affect other things. For example, you do not want attendance to shorten the time you have scheduled just after the meeting for another task, say to finalise writing a report, and end up with that going out in an inadequate state and failing to meet its objective.

THE PEOPLE

Once you have a clear objective and agenda you can consider the people who should or should not attend. Generally speaking, the more who are present, the longer things will take. Think about:

- Who has to be there.
- Who might find it useful.
- Who should observe.
- Who has something positive to contribute.
- Who has an axe to grind.
- Who will make unnecessary problems and dilute effectiveness.

Sometimes the list of attendees is pre-ordained: it's the Board, the heads of department or everyone on a planning committee. Otherwise the job is to assemble the right group in a considered manner, matching expertise with the topic to be discussed. Beware of certain people being added to the list because of wrong influences; office politics, favours, democracy, and social factors, for instance. The group which meets must be able to make whatever decisions are necessary and everyone present should have a clear and positive reason for being there. You also need to think about who will do what. Who will be "in the Chair"? (More on this later.) Who will take notes, act as Secretary or, afterwards, prepare the minutes? Key roles need to be decided in advance, right down to who will organise any necessary refreshments.

A final point here: one aspect of pre-meeting preparation that may be necessary (and we will return to this for both Chair and participants in Chapters 2 and 3) is pre-meeting meetings. This is, I hope, not double-Dutch but a way of describing the getting together in twos, threes or whatever that is sometimes useful to plan joint strategies so as to act in accord on the day. Such preliminaries can have a powerful effect on the way a meeting runs. This may be positive or negative; sometimes such sessions will make a meeting shorter and more constructive; an alliance can see matters agreed promptly or alternatively it can represent an attempt at manipulation. Whichever the case may be, it is important to:

- Never underestimate the importance of pre-meeting preparation or assume others will not be doing it.
- Take time yourself to form the necessary alliances.
- Watch for signs of other such alliances and anticipate their effect on the meeting.

Bear in mind also that both visible and invisible alliances can be useful, although some that are thought to be invisible may well be revealed on the day.

THE MEETING ENVIRONMENT
Everything – even the room and location – acts in some way to influence how a meeting will go. The hazards are many and include:

- Too many people in too small a room;
- Too little light or air;
- Uncomfortable chairs;
- No visual aids when these would be useful;
- Interruptions, which can range from a badly-timed tea break (i.e. one that happens just as things are starting to flow) to the now

ubiquitous mobile phone (do insist they are switched off – even silent texting is a huge distraction to both the person doing it and everyone else).

At least the old hazard of a smoky room has been outlawed by recent legislation, though some will want smoking breaks and that needs to be coped with too. Some thought is certainly necessary if such hazards are to be avoided. Plan to hold your meeting in the right place, with the right surroundings and equipment – "right" meaning anything that will act positively to make sure things go well. Choose, for example, a meeting place that is:

- Quiet (if possible, without a telephone);
- Private (if necessary);
- Sufficiently spacious;
- Equipped with the required number of power points;
- Comfortable, with suitable chairs;
- Well-ventilated so that people do not freeze, sweat or doze off;
- Pleasant, or with a suitable ambience (this is not necessarily a luxury – people will be less able to think creatively if they are unhappy with their surroundings).

There is an old military saying that time spent in reconnaissance is seldom wasted. So too with all the preliminaries dealt with in this chapter. Meetings are important. A great deal can depend on their going well – everything from reputations to large amounts of money. It is therefore important to create a sound foundation for the meeting process.

There are major factors here, such as agendas and objectives; and results are not helped if details are missed, if someone disappears from a meeting "to get a pencil" just as it starts.

Next on our agenda is the question of who is the Chair, and how this helps to ensure a constructive meeting. Note that there is good advice for everyone in the next chapter even if you do not (yet?) find yourself Chairing meetings.

One more thing …
It seems ubiquitous in many meetings for visual aids to be used, though

there are some where they are not, and where they would not be appropriate; although on other occasions the lack of them can dilute effectiveness. Most often this means PowerPoint slides. The phrase "death by PowerPoint" is now firmly in the language and nothing makes for a worse meeting experience than someone reading dense text off a screen showing endless slides, while looking over their shoulder and away from the group. (As a totally biased recommendation, if you are keen to avoid this form of meeting "death", check out my book *The PowerPoint Detox*).

We will return to the use of visual aids later; here let's note only that their preparation, and the time it takes to make a good job of them, must be scheduled in before the meeting (and not done in a rush two minutes before a meeting starts).

Chapter 2

LEADING MEETINGS:
The role of an effective Chair

A true leader is one who designs cathedrals and then shares the vision that inspires others to build it.
Jan Carlzon

Somewhere in Shakespeare's *Much Ado About Nothing* there is the line "When two men ride of a horse, one must sit behind". So it is with meetings; even with the less formal ones, someone has to be in charge. That does not necessarily imply that whoever is "in the Chair" should be the most senior person present or should do most of (or even lead) the talking. What it does imply is that he or she should be responsible for directing the meeting, and directing it purposefully towards goals known to all the participants.

Every meeting should therefore have a "Chair" (though they may need no official tag). An appropriate person is needed, because the role is important and may be substantial. Don't choose just anyone – "Why don't you lead, John; Mary did it last time we met." An effectively conducted Chairing role can ensure a well-directed meeting, and this in turn can mean that:

● The meeting will focus better on its objectives.
● Discussion can be more constructive.
● A thorough review can be ensured so that ad hoc decisions are avoided.

- All sides of the argument or case can be reflected upon and weighed in the balance.
- Proceedings can be kept businesslike and less argumentative (even when dealing with contentious issues).

As we will see, all the results of effective Chairing are positive and, as a result, likely to make for an effective meeting. Put succinctly, a good Chairperson will lead the meeting, handle the discussion, and see that objectives are met – promptly, efficiently, effectively and without wasting time.

THE RIGHT PERSON

As has been said, this is an important role. The choice of who exactly will be in the chair must reflect the responsibilities that the task entails. Steps need to be taken from the beginning to get a suitable person in the chair, and get participants to accept the need for someone to be in charge – to see it as something practical that will help everyone. To state the obvious, an ordered meeting will be likely to achieve more than one where chaos reigns.

At this point, let's flag two simple yet key rules that any Chairperson must stick to (and which any group of people meeting should always respect). They are, very simply:

- Only one person may talk at a time.
- And the Chairperson decides who (should this be necessary).

Already, this should begin to make you think about who will make a good Chairperson. The following checklist of responsibilities lays out the full picture.

THE LEADER'S RESPONSIBILITIES

The list that follows illustrates the range and nature of the tasks involved. It also shows clearly that there are skills required, perhaps skills that must be studied, learned and practiced. Whoever is leading the meeting must:

- Command the respect of those attending (and if they do not know

27

them, then such respect must be won rapidly by the way they are seen to operate).

- Do their homework and come prepared (i.e. having read any relevant documents and taken any other action necessary to help them take charge. They should also encourage others to do the same, as good preparation makes for more considered and succinct contributions to the meeting).
- Be on time.
- Start (and finish) on time.
- Ensure any administrative matters are well organised and will be taken care of appropriately (for example refreshments and, if it is necessary, the matter of taking minutes, the details of which are reviewed on page 85).
- Start on the right note and lead into the agenda.
- Introduce people if necessary (and certainly know who's who themselves – name cards can help everyone at some meetings).
- Set, explain and keep people to the rules, and do so fairly and consistently.
- Control the discussion, and do so in light of the various people who may be present: the talkative, the strident and so on.
- Encourage individual contributions where appropriate or necessary.
- Ask questions to clarify comments made where necessary. It is important to query anything unclear and do so at once. This can save time and argument, whereas if the meeting runs on with something being misinterpreted then it will become a muddle and take longer to reach any conclusion.
- Ensure everyone has their say.
- Act to keep the discussion to the point.
- Listen (as in LISTEN) if the Chair has missed things then the chances of the meeting proceeding smoothly are low and it may deteriorate into "But you said …" arguments; everyone needs to do this, and a non-listening Chair sets a bad example as well as putting themselves in a poor position to conduct a good meeting. The box, right, goes into more detail and shows how listening is an active process – for everyone involved in a meeting.
- Watch the clock. Remind others to do the same and manage the timing and any time pressure along the way.

- Summarise, clearly and succinctly; something that must usually be done regularly, perhaps item by item.
- Cope with any upsets, outbursts and emotion.
- Provide the final word. The Chair should summarise and bring matters to a conclusion. Similarly, link to any final administrative detail, such as setting the date for the subsequent action or further meeting(s).
- See (after the meeting ends) to any follow-up action. This may be especially important when there is a series of sessions: people promise something at one and turn up at the next having done little or nothing about it. Some chasing in between may well be part of the job.

All this must be done with patience, goodwill, good humour and respect, not only for all those present (and maybe others) but also for the objectives of the meeting. Now let us turn to a number of factors worth investigating in more detail as they directly affect how a meeting works.

CHECKLIST: Effective listening.

Of course you listen. Really? Never had a breakdown in communications because you did not really take something in properly? Honestly? If you want to demonstrate to yourself how listening varies in effectiveness, just consider what happens when someone says something that you disagree with. At once your mind begins to spend some of its power not on listening but on developing a counter argument. The effect of this can be pronounced.

Not only do you want to take in clearly everything that is said to you in a meeting, you want to appear to be a good listener, one who takes the proceedings seriously. The checklist that follows sets out some principles that are useful and which certainly show listening to be an active process. So, you should:

- Want to listen: recognising how it can help you is the first step to doing it well.

- Look like a good listener: let people see that they have your attention by appropriate eye contact and acknowledgement of what is said to you.
- Listen and stop talking: you cannot do both at once, the meeting will become awkward and you need to resist the temptation to interrupt, waiting until the point is fully made (or what you do will seem like evasion).
- Use empathy: put yourself in the other person's shoes, try to see things from their point-of-view and make it clear you are doing so.
- Check: clarify as you go along if anything is not clear, and note that leaving doing so too long can simply build up bigger problems later.
- Remain calm: concentrate on the facts and try not to let overreaction, or becoming emotional, hinder your ability to take in the full message.
- Concentrate: and allow nothing to distract you.
- Focus on key points: get to the nub of what is being said, which may be buried in other, less important, information and comment.
- Avoid personalities: concentrate on what is said – the argument – rather than who is saying it.
- Take one thing at a time: jumping ahead, especially if you do so only on the basis of assumption, can cause problems.
- Avoid pointed reactions: certainly initially; hear the comment out and do not look horrified or ecstatic (even if you are!) ahead of working out how you intend to proceed given whatever comments prompted the feeling.
- Make notes: do not trust your memory, jot down key points as the meeting proceeds (and, if you feel it is polite or necessary, ask permission to do so). Sometimes this needs to be done for all to see, on, say, a flipchart.

There is an old saying that people have two ears and one mouth for a good reason; certainly we should always remember that listening is just as important as speaking. Furthermore, listening is not just important to meetings; it is a career skill, one that affects how you are perceived and is worth taking care with in many contexts.

Getting off to a good start
The best meetings start well, continue well, and end well. A good start helps set the scene, and this too is the responsibility of whoever is the Chair. So, it works best to start the meeting in a way that:

- Is positive.
- Makes its purpose, timing (and any procedure) clear.
- Establishes the Chairperson's authority and right to be in charge.
- Creates the right atmosphere (which may differ depending on whether it is to prompt creative thinking or, say, undertake detailed analysis of figures).
- Generates interest and enthusiasm for what is to come (yes, even if it is seen as a tedious regular review).
- Is immediately perceived as professional and businesslike.

It may also help if the Chairperson involves others early on, rather than beginning with a lengthy monologue. This takes us to the next point.

Prompting discussion
Of course, there are meetings where prompting contributions is the least of the Chairperson's problems. But if you are in the Chair you will want contributions from everyone (why otherwise did you invite them to attend?). So, to ensure that you get adequate and representative discussion, and to ensure that subsequent decisions are made on all the appropriate facts and information, you may need to prompt discussion.

Sometimes, there are specific reasons why meeting participants hold back. They may, for example:

- Fear rejection or the reaction of others to the points they might make.
- Feel pressure from other, perhaps more senior or more powerful, people.
- Lack preparation (and possibly as a result an appreciation of the objectives).
- Have an incomplete understanding of what has gone on earlier.

Alternatively, they may simply lack any encouragement to make contributions. A good Chairperson will ask for views, and do so in a way that prompts open, considered comments. But note that it is sometimes easy to skew comments (wittingly or not) by the tone or manner with which they are called for. For instance, a senior manager is unlikely to encourage creative suggestions if he or she fields a personal thought first, particularly if it puts their view up front: "I think is a good idea, what do others think?". This risks effectively forcing agreement rather than constructive critique, which might be far more useful. A worse version of this sort of thing is the comment, "It is only a suggestion, but bear in mind who's making it," and the worst of all is a Chairperson who uses the phrase, "When I want your opinion, I'll give it to you"! Clearly, such an attitude is not a recipe for success.

Be careful not to load the dice in this way. Much comment-prompting will come through questions.

Questioning techniques

Questions must of course be clear. Remember also that there are two kinds of question: open and closed, with open questions more likely to prompt discussion (this is explored in more detail in the box below, together with the concept of probing questions).

The foundation of questioning techniques

Three types of question can be used:

- Closed questions: these are questions that can be answered easily with a quick "Yes" or "No". As such, they are most useful for checking facts and leading into deeper areas of investigation. But, otherwise, their use may be limited, especially when a fuller answer is sought.
- Open questions: these cannot be answered with a simple "Yes" or "No". They are designed to get people talking, to elucidate real information and detail – they typically start with the words: what, why, when, where, how and who and with phrases such as, "Tell me about ....." (this may not technically be a question, but does get people talking).

The difference between these two approaches is marked. If someone asks, "Will I be able to take on new things next year?" (or specifies a particular area of work), the answer may well be "Yes". But if the conversation then moves on, there is little they have really discovered. When will a new involvement start? How will it be initiated? What will it involve? And so on. However, if they ask "Can you tell me something about any new involvements you see me taking on next year, please?" the subsequent conversation may explain much more.

● Probing questions: sometimes even an open question does not produce everything you want. Then you need to be prepared to pursue a point, asking a series of probing questions to focus on a particular area and get to the required level of detail. Phrases like "Tell me more about .... ?" or "Can you explain that further?" can make a good start.

Questions are of major significance. Have good ones ready and do not be afraid to refer to them ("There were specific questions I wanted to ask about this, let me just check"); doing so is evidence of being well prepared.

The circumstances will affect how questions are best asked. Discussion can be prompted around the meeting in numbers of ways, primarily in the following six:

1. Overhead questions: these are put to the meeting as a whole, left for whoever picks them up to answer and are useful for starting discussion.

2. Overhead/directed questions: these are put to the whole meeting (as above) and either followed immediately by the same question to an individual, or after a pause as a way of overcoming lack of response: "Now, what do we all think about this? ... David?"

3. Direct to an individual: direct to a (named) individual without preliminaries; useful to get an individual reaction or check understanding.

4. Rhetorical: a question demanding no answer can still be a good way to make a point or prompt thinking and the Chairperson can provide a response if they wish.

5. Re-directed: this presents a question asked of the Chair straight back to the meeting either as an overhead or direct question: "Good question. What do we all think? David?"

6. Development question: this really gets discussion going, it builds on the answer to an earlier question and moves it round the meeting: "So, Mary thinks it will take too long; do we see any other problems?"

Prompting discussion is as important as control. It is the only way of making sure the meeting is well balanced and takes in all required points of view. If decisions are made in the absence of this, someone may be back to you later saying something like: "This is just not acceptable. My department never really got a chance to make their case."

Because of this, it may sometimes be necessary to persevere to be sure to get all the desired comment the meeting needs. Ways have to be found to achieve this; two examples are:

• Asking again: as simple as that. Rephrase the question (perhaps it was not understood originally) and ensure the point is clear and that people know a comment is required

• Use silence: the trouble is that silence can be embarrassing. But even a short silence to make it clear you will wait for an answer may be sufficient to get someone speaking. So do not rush on, after all maybe the point deserves a moment's thought before anyone says anything. Wait ... and contributions will come.

Concentrate

A good, serious meeting demands concentration. It is the job of whoever is in the Chair to assist achieving this in them and in others. Beware of interruptions. Organise to deal with messages, mobile telephones or simply the refreshments arriving in mid-meeting as all delay proceedings and ensure concentration is lost.

It helps therefore if:

- Rules are laid down about messages.
- Breaks are organised (for longer sessions) so that people know how they can deal with messages etc, and as a way of helping to maintain concentration.
- Refreshments are organised in advance (or for before or after the meeting).
- Others outside the meeting (including switchboard operators, secretaries and others) are briefed as to how matters should be handled. It is as bad for a key customer, say, to be told: "Sorry, they're in a meeting," as for a meeting to be interrupted; perhaps worse, so deciding priorities is important.
- If there are unforeseen interruptions then do not compete with them while peoples' attention is elsewhere. Wait, deal with them – then continue, recapping if necessary.

Concentration is vital for everyone in a meeting, and, of course needs to be focused on the right things within the meeting. Do not be side tracked, beware of digressions, beware of running a meeting within a meeting, sometimes you will unearth separate issues that arc worth noting to either pursue or investigate on some other occasion.

Keep order
Sometimes even the best planned and organised meeting gets out of hand. So, here it is worth noting some further key rules for the Chair:

- Never get upset or emotional yourself.
- Pick on one element of what is being expressed and try to isolate and deal with that without heat; and thus reduce the overall temperature.
- Agree (at least with the sentiments of any outburst) before regrouping: "You are right, this is a damned difficult issue, and emotions are bound to run high. Now let's take one thing at a time."

If these approaches do not work you may have to take more drastic action, for example:

- Call for a few minutes complete silence before attempting to move on.

- Call for a short break, and insist it is taken without discussion continuing.
- Put the problem item on one side until later (though be sure to specify how and when it will be dealt with, and then make sure you do what was agreed).
- Abandon the meeting until another time (which should be agreed and scheduled).

This last option is clearly a last resort, but ultimately may be better than allowing disorder to continue. Usually, a firm stand made as soon as any sort of unrest occurs will meet the problem head on, nip it in the bud and allow it to be dealt with. Whatever happens, as it said in *The Hitchhikers' Guide to the Galaxy*: DON'T PANIC.

I would not want to give the impression that chairing meetings is all drama, however, so let us end this chapter with something more constructive.

SPARKING CREATIVITY

It is said that whereas managers are not paid to have all the good ideas needed to keep their department (or whatever) running effectively, they are paid to make sure there are sufficient ideas to keep it ahead. As a result many meetings need to be creative. Two heads really can be better than one, and several can, if correctly orchestrated, be better still. Yet new ideas can also prompt a negative cycle all too easily. Such discussion can spiral into a tit for tat of "your idea's no good" or "mine's better" – with scoring points taking precedence over giving new ideas a chance.

This is another thing that the Chairperson has to deal with: needing to foster creative thinking and open-mindedness to ensure that instant negative responses and reasons to disagree do not become the order of the day. The Chairperson must therefore:

- Actively stimulate creative thinking (and should make it clear that this is part of the meeting, and rule against anyone who instantly rejects ideas without first considering them).

- Personally contribute new ideas or steer the discussion in new, or unusual, directions.
- Find new ways of looking at things.
- Consider novel approaches and give them a chance.
- Aim to solve problems, not tread familiar pathways.

Some groups who meet regularly get better and better at this. But this does not usually happen spontaneously; more often, it is the result of someone putting together the right team and prompting them not only to think along certain lines but also always to remain open-minded above all else.

Acting to prompt creativity

People are often innately creative – given the opportunity. This opportunity may be no more than asking – "what do you think? ... any ideas?" Good managers do this as a matter of routine, believing that their role is to find – prompt – the ideas needed to carry their operation forward, not necessarily to have them all themselves.

In such circumstances people develop a feeling of confidence and come to believe that they can be creative. Conversely, if they are never asked or consulted they may come to believe that this is because they really do have nothing to offer. Sometimes a long-term "campaign" is necessary to build confidence and this can be an important thread in keeping in touch with and involving staff.

If you manage other people, then here is a method of generating thinking (and saving yourself time and developing others), the deployment of which is literally invaluable. Imagine: a head comes round your door and someone says something like, "I'm not sure about this, can you spare a moment to go through it?" As a caring manager maybe you clear a few minutes (then or later). More often a busy manager is likely to be tempted to focus primarily on minimising the interruption. They look or listen and respond with a quick comment, often virtually an instruction, to "do it this way". A better response throws it straight back to the staff member, saying, "What do you think makes sense here?" or something similar, which can be used to get people thinking. They may ask for time, or discussion may continue there and then as they pose some alternatives. In which case the manager must insist and act to prompt people in the right direction. "Fine, but what do you think makes best sense in this instance?" The consistent use of this approach will quickly become recognised. People, understanding that they are not going to get an instant answer, will give things some thought first, though they may still check it with the manager. Variations are possible. A different response to such a question would be to get two staff members into constructive discussion: "Have a word with John and let me know what you work out" (perhaps identifying why John, or whoever, is suitable). This process, which can develop into a short meeting, may take a little longer than an instant "do this" response but it will:

- Save time in the longer term by developing the right habits.
- Develop self-sufficiency (witness how people usually make the right decision when you are not there to ask and they have to act alone).
- Spur creative thinking and new ideas either by the individual concerned or through their discussion with you or others.

All this is useful, and thus worth the short digression, but as well as the kind of interaction described, many meetings need to be creative (indeed the situation above can be linked to a meeting, for instance with a manager asking someone to think about something and then speak about at the next departmental meeting).

If the need is to discover new ways of doing something, overcome a problem or identify new opportunities, then a meeting must do just that. Meetings always need to be constructive, and they often also benefit from being creative. Groups that act to drive towards this find they get better and better at it; creativity becomes a habit. Sometimes constructive, idea-focused discussion is all that is necessary. On occasions, something more is necessary and the prime technique here, one certainly worth a word, is brainstorming. This is a misunderstood term and for some implies anarchy; in fact, it only works if organized systematically.

Brainstorming
This is a group activity and can be used to provide an almost instant

burst of idea generation. It needs a prescribed approach and like all meetings someone must take the role of facilitator or Chair. They should:

- Gather people around and explain the objectives.
- Explain that there are to be no comments on ideas at the first stage.
- Allow a little time for thought (singly or, say, in pairs).
- Start taking contributions and noting them down (publicly, on say a flipchart).
- When a good sized list is established analysis can begin.
- Grouping similar ideas together can make the list more manageable.
- Open-minded discussion can then review the list.
- Identify ideas that can be taken forward.

Such a session must exclude the word "impossible" from the conversation, at least initially (and especially when used in senses such as, "It's impossible, we don't do things that way," (why not?) or, "It's impossible, we tried it and it didn't work" (how long ago and in what form?).

By avoiding negative or censorious first responses, by allowing one idea to spark another and variations on a theme to refine a point (perhaps taking it from wild to practical), you can produce genuinely new approaches. It can be fun to do, satisfying in outcome and time-efficient to undertake – and a group who brainstorms regularly get quicker and more certain in their production of good, useable, ideas. Try it: you might be surprised at the results.

No more may be necessary, but some people feel that an exercise – what is called an ice-breaker – can help kick start the process. These range widely and may often be linked to the topic to be discussed, and certainly to the group or organisation involved. As a simple example, consider a meeting held to find ways of improving the rather over-officious nature of written communication (to, say, customers). Giving people an example and asking them to rewrite it so that it is humorous will start the session by getting people bringing some fresh thinking to bear (what modern jargon calls "thinking outside the box"). In this case only fresh thinking will allow the task to be done the prescribed way and it sets the scene for what comes next. Such a process can involve people individually (writing their version) and as a group (reading out what is written, critique and perhaps – to add spice – ranking what is done).

Other exercises can be more elaborate.

Lateral thinking

What may seem to be real digressions from a meeting or just a bit of fun can also be useful, not so much to literally spark creativity as to get people in the right mood and thinking constructively.

Some of the exercises that constitute such sessions are very much part of organisational folklore. Perhaps the best example of this is the Boat Game. A group must imagine they are out at sea in a boat which will sink, drowning everyone, unless some of the occupants are thrown out. Participants can be themselves, or sometimes take on a famous persona, and must suggest why they should be saved and why others should be cast out. There is, of course, no right answer, but it can be fun and people's thinking is certainly led away from routine.

Other such "games" do have an answer, though finding the answer demands some lateral thinking. By way of example, my favourite is a classic one revolving round the story of a poor peasant in debt to a rich landowner. Unable to pay he pleads for an alternative. The rich landowner tells him he will take his daughter as a slave and, faced with starvation for the whole family, he lets the girl go. Later, racked with guilt, he goes to the estate of the rich landowner to plead for her release. Sadistically, the landowner suggests a test: in front of his whole household he takes a bag and says he will put one black and one white stone into it – if the girl can pick out the white one she can go free, otherwise she must stay for life. He stoops to the gravel path, which consists of a mixture of black and white stones, and puts two in the bag. Only the daughter sees that he has cheated, selecting two black stones to ensure she cannot win.

The question that the group must answer is – how can the girl secure her freedom?

This kind of exercise can certainly prompt lateral thinking and set the mood for later idea generation. In case you want a moment to think about this, the answer is given on page 42.

Other aspects of meeting procedure and practice have a bearing here, but let us conclude by stressing again the influence of the choice of the Chairperson, the nature of that role and the way it is carried out. Without someone at the helm as it were, any meeting risks running onto the rocks.

In the next chapter we shall look at the question of attending meetings: what, as a participant, can you contribute to, and get from, meetings? There are also more lessons here even if you are normally the Chair.

Answer to the question posed on page 40: When the girl is made to pick and pull out a stone she pretends to drop it accidentally. She then suggests that they look at the remaining stone – if it is white then clearly she must have picked the black and must remain a prisoner, if it is black she must have picked the white and won her freedom. The crowd readily agree and the landowner, feeling he cannot be seen to have cheated, reluctantly agrees too. She takes out the remaining stone which is of course black and, with a trick cleverer than her captor, obtains her release.

Chapter 3

ATTENDING MEETINGS:
How play your part effectively

One should not aim at being possible to understand, but at being impossible to misunderstand.
Quintillian (Roman rhetorician)

Meetings can waste time, money and effort – not least your time, money and effort. But the benefits of a good meeting in terms of ideas, debate, decision, and communication are considerable, as has already been mentioned. Perhaps we should all resolve never to go to a meeting unless we are convinced that it is likely to be genuinely constructive and useful. Specifically, every time a meeting beckons you must ask yourself:

- What can I contribute?
- What can I get from it?

Come to definite answers to both questions. This means considering alternatives: instead of going yourself, can you submit a note, read the minutes afterwards, or delegate someone else to attend? Make a conscious decision about attending: unless there is a three-line whip, make sure you really feel it is necessary.

THE BASIS OF MAKING PARTICIPATION EFFECTIVE
Once you have decided to attend you can consider how to make doing

so worthwhile: after all, meetings are no exception to the old saying that you only get out of things what you put in. Overall, the key things that make for effective participation in meetings are:

- Sound preparation: you have to know what will be discussed and why, be ready for it, and have done your homework.
- Your personal meeting profile: this goes closely with communicating effectively, but also raises separate issues about how what you say will be taken.
- Effective communication: you have to judge and decide the best way to contribute: that is what you say and how you say it (and for that matter what you will not say); and perhaps also exactly when you will say it.
- Well-handled discussion. You have to be not only ready to make prepared contributions but also to think quickly on your feet as it were in order to respond appropriately to the contributions of others or requests from the Chair. In other words, you have to be able to put your case effectively not just in isolation but so that it surfaces – and sticks – through what may be a maelstrom of comment.

One other point is worth a short digression here – you may need to look the part. Although I would not presume to tell you how to dress, you may be involved in circumstances where this is worth a moment's thought. For example, perhaps you are to attend a meeting where not everyone will know you, or perhaps there is some other factor that will make your appearance important. If you rush in late, unkempt, and clutching a collapsing pile of files you will certainly not give the desired impression. Dress codes vary around the world and between organisations, but perhaps the best advice is always to be a little better dressed than the average. You could do worse than to consider the impression you want to make: presumably, that of someone who is well-prepared, efficient, authoritative, expert, well-informed, credible, or whatever. You can compile your own version of such a list: you know what is important in your own circles and in your own organisation.

Seating is important in the same regard. Do not try to command a meeting from around a corner or out on a limb; sit where you can be seen and from where you can communicate effectively. This consideration may need to relate to particular people. Will you be able to catch the eye of whoever is in the Chair? Where will you be in relationship to someone whose support or opposition you expect? And if it is your meeting, give some forethought to the seating – for instance, would a round table work well for some meetings? Do you need to place people specifically (using name cards, perhaps)?

Now, back to the four principles identified previously.

SOUND PREPARATION

Ensuring that you get the right message over needs some thought and well-considered action. This starts, unsurprisingly, with preparation. The first rule is simple: always prepare; you must have a real familiarity with the matter in hand. You will never make your point well if you try to do so off the top of your head. The second rule is: horses for courses. Meetings vary and the amount of preparation you need to do will vary likewise (and will not necessarily relate directly to, say, the length of the meeting). Sometimes preparation requires only a couple of minutes' thought, sometimes a day's work (and everything in between). The key areas involved include the need to:

- Read anything necessary in advance. This might include past minutes, agendas, documents, reports, proposals and memos that have been circulated and that have a bearing on the meeting. It might also include background reading or research – including discussions with others – to familiarise yourself with a topic (perhaps with the aim to do so better than other participants).

- Annotate any relevant documents to highlight key issues and make your own notes as necessary. It is essential to be able to check facts fast at a meeting. You do not impress people by fumbling through a pile of papers, saying, "I know it's here somewhere."

- Note who else will attend so that your plans take into account their roles and positions. For example, is anyone attending on whom you can rely for support – or is it yours that will be relied on?

- Plan any questions that you will need to ask as the meeting progresses. Sometimes you may need to plan exactly how you will ask them.

- Prepare your contribution. This is necessary when the situation is more formal (it may be almost like a presentation). Make sure that you have thought things through and have any necessary notes of what you need to say and how you will put it over.

In general make notes of anything you will need to know, say, or do. It is no good trusting to your memory and then coming out of the meeting saying, "I just wish I had said…" Often when the moment has passed, it's passed and either it is difficult or impossible to return to the matter you have missed. A meeting may well be a one-off opportunity.

On the day, all sorts of difficulties can conspire to make what you want to do more difficult. People may not listen as attentively as you want (and, no doubt, feel you deserve). Or they may stick doggedly to their current views and the status quo, and find it difficult to be convinced of your arguments. There may also be any number of other pressures; time constraints, an emergency of some kind, or other issues might arise that threaten to thwart your intentions, however well rehearsed.

All of this goes to prove the point: preparation is vital, and time spent on it can make all the difference between a good meeting and a complete waste of time. It is important to get it right: many meeting have a great deal riding on them and hoping to wing it is rarely a sensible option.

Controlling your nerves

However well you have prepared for your meeting, you are unlikely to succeed in your intentions if (as has already been said) you fail to communicate successfully during it. Before looking in detail at the principles involved in getting your point across, it is worth mentioning something that can derail you at the start: nerves. Meetings can be daunting occasions, all the more so if they are especially important, if you are the most junior person there, or if you have to stand up and make a formal presentation. The additional factors involved in presentations are beyond the brief for this book, but it may be a topic to investigate separately. Indeed, if presentation is not your bag then it may be essential to do so; bear in mind that mostly lacklustre presentations are the result of not knowing enough about what makes them work – anyone can make a workmanlike one if they do some homework

Once again, preparation is the best antidote for nerves: you'll feel less nervous if you are clear about what you want to say and do. Simple practical measures may also be useful, ranging from a deep breath to a sip of water (avoid fashionable fizzy water, incidentally, as it can have side effects). It is usually no problem to have some notes in front of you if this helps. "Stage fright" is not, however, entirely negative: the adrenaline that it produces is a stimulus that can be useful.

YOUR MEETING PROFILE

Every organisation has an image. The only question is whether this just happens, for good or ill, or if it is seen as something to actively create, maintain and make positive. Similarly, every time you open your mouth in a meeting then, as well as what you say, the process of your saying it says something about you. Whether you like it or not this is true. And it matters. The profile, like your appearance, wittingly or unwittingly presented may influence whether people believe, trust or like you. It may influence how they feel about your expertise, or whether they can see themselves agreeing with you or 'doing business' with you.

Your personal profile is not only an influence in your job, one that links to the objectives you have, it also potentially affects your career. Surely it is unavoidable that, given the profusion of meetings with which most people are involved, how you come over progressively typecasts you in the eyes of others – including your boss – as the sort of person who is to be reckoned with, is going places, or not.

It bears thinking about

Certainly acting to influence your prevailing style, and what your meeting contributions say about you, is worth thinking about. If there is an inevitable sub text of this sort, you cannot afford to let it go by default, you need to consciously influence it. Start by considering what you want people to think of you. Take a simple point. You want to be thought of as efficient. Then the style you adopt must surely say something about this. If it is right, it assists effective communication, and certainly if you then cover everything you said you would, then a sense of efficiency surely follows. The same applies to many characteristics: being seen as knowledgeable, experienced, authoritative and so on. All such characteristics are worth considering to ascertain exactly how you can achieve the effect you want. Such images are cumulative. They build up over time and can assist in the establishment and maintenance of relationships. Whether this is with a colleague or concerned with establishing with your boss that you are a good person to work with (as well as good at your work) then the influence can be powerful. Thus, a good performance at one meeting makes it more likely that you will be taken seriously at the next.

Such images are not created in a moment or with a word. There is more to appearing honest than saying: Let me be completely honest (which might actually just ring alarm bells!). If people are to respect and take notice of you then everything about the way you come over is important. This is so in routine circumstances and assumes added importance if you are amongst a group more senior or experienced than you; you do not want to be taken as the poor relation. All this means that every detail that influences your meeting contributions is important; after all, you may have just two or three minutes to make a point and a great deal could hang on how it goes across.

Here, let me also suggest that you might have in mind a list of characteristics you want actively to avoid seeming to embrace. For example, appearing dogmatic, patronising, inflexible, old fashioned, or whatever, in your approach might do you little good. Some other characteristics are sometimes to be emphasised, sometimes not. Stubbornness is a good example. To cultivate a truly professional persona you need to be clearly understood (a factor we return to later) in addition it helps if you:

- Speak at a slightly slower rate than normal: you do not need to overdo this and slow down so that you appear to be half a-s-l-e-e-p. But pace is important and any nervousness can make you rush or, at worst, gabble. A considered pace – not least one implying a considered view – will be more likely to allow things to be made clear, and misunderstandings avoided. It allows people to keep up; particularly for example when it is clear they may be wanting to make a note: you can slow down especially for that. In addition, too rapid fire a delivery can sound glib and promote a lack of trust. It is important not to sound like a dodgy second-hand car dealer, who will always go at a rate that precludes easy interruption. Also rapidity can allow key points to be missed; and, in any case, what you promote may need all the weight possible.

- Make inflection work for you: inflection is what makes, for example, a question mark stand out at the end of a sentence, and also what gives variety and interest to the way you speak. It is important that intended inflection is noticed.

- Smile: not a fixed grin, of course, not even an obviously visible smile, but a pleasant demeanor produces a pleasant tone and this does make for the right sound. A warm tone of voice produces a feeling that the you are efficient, helpful and, most important, have empathy with other participants.

- Enthuse: there are many situations when enthusiasm is important; indeed enthusiasm is about the only good thing in life that is contagious. If you are passionate about a point or case, this must show.

- Be positive: this goes hand in hand with enthusiasm. Avoid saying 'possibly', 'maybe' and 'I think', when you should give definitive information – It is … – to make your point.

- Get the emphasis right: it is necessary to get the emphasis right in terms of both words – "this is *really* important," or "this is *really important*" – and in terms of the parts of your message that most need it.

- Be concise: most of the people with whom you will find yourself in meetings, at whatever level, will expect and appreciate it if you value their time. This especially means that convoluted descriptions (and inappropriate jargon, especially if it needs explaining) need to be thought about in advance, and made concise yet precise – succinct is a good word to bear in mind. Be careful with the social chat. It is often easily picked up by others, but there can be a thin line between introducing a welcome digression and becoming seen as a time waster who threatens the agenda.

- Personalise: use names where appropriate. This is especially effective in a group where you do not know everyone. An early task may be to make a note showing where people are sitting as introductions occur and then make accurate references to people thereafter. Everyone likes a personal touch.

Your intended profile will come, in part, from specifics such as choice of words, but also from the whole way in which you use language. So it is to the essentials of clear communication and more about the use of language that we now move on.

EFFECTIVE COMMUNICATION

There are occasions when the desire to transfer information is frustrated by the circumstances, which compounds problems and puts recipients in danger of failing to perceive your point. If you are puzzling over that last sentence (and that would not be surprising), let me rephrase it: communication is not easy. Never assume it is easy. Always think about the best way to make even a seemingly simple point. It was the late US President Richard Nixon who is usually credited with the remark, "I know you believe you understand what you think I said, but I am not sure you realise what you heard is not what I meant". There is a serious point here and I suspect you do not need to have attended many meetings to have seen poor communication in action.

There are several factors that will help you communicate successfully at a meeting.

Stick to the rules

Following a few basic rules will help you and everyone present (and at least they will prevent the meeting from deteriorating into a shouting match). So do not:

- Monopolise the conversation.
- Constantly interrupt others.
- Become emotional or argumentative to no good purpose.
- Make it difficult to stick to the allotted time.
- Appear unprepared, undisciplined, or a troublemaker.
- Digress pointlessly from the topic.

Overall, the aim is to try to use the Chairperson and any agreed procedure in order to play your part in creating an orderly meeting. Doing so in an orderly manner can see you standing out positively in face of another's undisciplined bluster.

It is, however, said that rules are made to be broken, and although it may be very much the exception to break them, there are occasions when the best tactic is to do just that, for example to use one of the following in a calculated way to make a strong point:

- A dramatic outburst.
- A fist banged on the table as you say "No!"
- A display of emotion, most useful positively to reinforce a point.
- Some (carefully chosen) humour, which can defuse a difficult situation or simply be used to get attention.
- Bad temper (although it must be controlled).
- An interruption (to cause a delay, perhaps).

Do not overdo it, or such tactics will quickly become self-defeating.

Stick to the structure
Often a meeting proceeds along lines dictated by the Chairperson or simply according to practicality. As each topic on the agenda comes up, a useful sequence is:

- Introduction: stating the reason for a given item, setting the scene, referring back to previous discussion, and spelling out the sub-agenda for the item.
- Setting out the issues: putting over points for and against, outlining key points (for example, costs, timing, staffing etc), describing both the main issues and any implications.
- Debate: developing other contributions into logical arguments and establishing for everyone that there is a basis upon which decisions can be made.
- Summary: pulling together of previous discussion and a look ahead to future action, communication, or decisions.

This sort of structure usually makes a good way to proceed. You can usefully use this to judge when to do what and take this to the point of labeling or signposting your intentions, saying, for example, "Let me summarise..." or "Let me just comment on the costs issue..." to make clear what you are doing, and perhaps effectively reserve the right to come back on other points.

Get your facts right

Perhaps this should go without saying, but meetings can spend an inordinately long time questioning, checking, or challenging facts. Where information proves incorrect, credibility can collapse (even, in fact, if the actual fact in contention was not key). This means you must take time to check, check, and check again. It also means that you must put information over in a way that is:

- Explicit: state things plainly, without obscuring them with irrelevances.
- Accurate: make sure your information is exactly right.
- Precise: choose carefully just the right piece of information to make the point.

I hope this does not sound pedantic. It matters, and an example may make clear how. Take figures, financial or otherwise, which often make an appearance at meetings. Say a cost is quoted as being "up 9.2 per cent", but that this proves inaccurate. Even if you say afterwards that you meant to say "about 9 per cent" is too late and does not undo the damage. Credibility will have been diluted just a bit – maybe an important bit – and the more decimal places are involved the more this shouts "accuracy"; though certainly remember that it is a nonsense to talk of "about 9.236%". This is an area for considerable care.

Always observe

Never get so set on what you are trying to say that you forget to note what others in the meeting are doing. After all, your comments will have to be fine-tuned in the light of your understanding of the state of the meeting. Take care to:

- Watch everything that goes on. See how people are reacting to the meeting (and to you) by observing their gestures and expressions – both are an important element of overall communication. Sometimes information available this way is subtle, or it may be more dramatic – with a loud snore from your left meaning that whoever is speaking has not succeed in generating the desired interest or enthusiasm.

- Listen attentively and actively. Make notes. Be seen to be listening. And never allow the Chairperson to respond to you by saying, "If you had been listening earlier, then…" (the checklist in Chapter 2 explores this).
- Use the information you pick up to finetune what you do. For example, one of the reasons comedy programmes have laughter tracks is that peoples' decision making – in this case about whether to laugh or not – is, in part, affected by others. Thus, if you see someone visibly agreeing with you then you might draw them in and get them to voice their support, or at least indicate their approval to others.

You will be able to make your points well only if you are in touch with the feeling of the meeting – constantly and accurately – throughout its course.

MAKING A POWERFUL POINT

In communications terms there are a number of things to achieve when you open your mouth at a meeting. You want people to listen, to believe that what you say is relevant, and ultimately for them to be prompted to agree or take action on a basis that reflects your views.

Thus the precise way in which you communicate is vital and worth getting right. Perhaps most of us have come out of a meeting disappointed because we failed to get a point over, and – worse – knowing that if we had described something better the results might well have been different. So, what you say needs to be understandable, attractive, and credible. Although what you say needs to come over in a cohesive way, these intentions must be injected individually and are worth reviewing separately first.

MAKE WHAT YOU SAY UNDERSTANDABLE

The difficulties of achieving clear understanding have already been referred to. Another point worth making here concerns what psychologists call cognitive cost. A general example will make this clear. Some instruction manuals (the ones for video recorders of old come to mind) have a similar effect whatever the page at which you open them; they seem to say the same thing – this is going to be difficult. They thus have, in the jargon, a high cognitive cost; in other words it is difficult to make head or tail of them and getting accurately to what they mean is hard work. So too with meetings: explain something in a disorganized ragged way and people resent it. More than that, if it's an idea they devalue it and may not even take it in as their minds wander. So, good clear description and explanation is far more than just a sensible courtesy. It says a lot about you and gives you a much better chance of receiving a fair and considered hearing; creating easy understanding is an opportunity to shine.

That said, here you should note a number of mechanisms that help to make sure that what you say is truly understood:

- Use clear signposts. In other words, tell people in advance how you will deal with something. (This is, incidentally, what I have just done by saying above that the key aims were to make what is said understandable, attractive and credible, then taking them one at a time). If people are clear about what is coming up, then they can see things in context and are more likely to want to listen. The same applies also to any subsidiary points, which can be presented with more signposting. You cannot really have too much of it.
- Have a clear structure. This is always important, even for brief remarks. The logic must be clear: a beginning, a middle, and an end are helpful. Whatever precise structure you choose, it must be appropriate – and signposted.
- Use the right sequence. This may take any form you like, for example one relating to the chronological order of events, but again exactly what you are doing should be spelt out and chosen to work sensibly, not so much for you but for those you address.
- Use visual aids. A picture really can be worth a thousand words. The time taken to produce a chart, diagram, graph or whatever can be well worthwhile (you then have to decide how to use it – as a slide, handout, or information displayed on a simple flipchart). More details about visual aids appears at the end of the next chapter.
- Avoid jargon. Or rather, use it carefully. It can be useful and comes in several varieties, for instance that of an organisation, an activity (for example, information technology) or specialist area (for example, engineering). It often abbreviates (as with AUJ – avoid

unnecessary jargon) and is only what might be called 'professional slang'. But it can also confuse, especially if you misjudge the level of technicality that is appropriate for a group. It needs watching because the use of jargon can become a reflex action – such a habit that sometimes you don't know you're doing it.

- Avoid gobbledegook. Nobody will take you seriously if you say "Considerable progress has been made in the preliminary work directed towards the establishment of the starting-point and initial activities", if what you mean is simply, "We are still trying to decide how to begin". Nor should you start every other sentence with the superfluous word "Basically..." or throw in words such as "proactive" when they add nothing; in any case, what is wrong with "active"?

- Don't describe just anything. Some things just cannot be described, at least on their own. Consider trying to tell someone how to tie a necktie. It is virtually impossible, but it is very easy to show someone. Never try to describe the impossible; use something – a picture, a diagram or whatever – in the form of a slide or handout to ensure that everyone is clear.

Remember, If you are not understood, nothing else will matter. Although few people will agree with something they do not understand, in meetings many are reluctant to actually say "I don't understand," for fear that it is they who will appear to be dense, so you will not always get feedback to allow correction. Create understanding as the foundation of everything else you do and you are off to a good start.

MAKE WHAT YOU SAY DESCRIPTIVE

It will be clear even to those with minimal experience of meetings that there is much more to them than simply telling people things: they will often need persuading. Indeed, they may need motivating, filling with enthusiasm, and more. This involves a whole area of different skills but here let's note that it is dependent on two key intentions. You must:

- Identify the needs of others and try to see things from their point-of-view, displaying appropriate empathy. If you understand their perspective you will be better placed to anticipate any objections and see what is likely to carry them with you.

- Put over a case that reflects this understanding and shows other people specifically, and if necessary individually, what your proposition is and, if necessary, how it will be better than other options.

For the moment let me just repeat that you should not believe you are there simply to tell people things – you are in fact doing something that is inherently more complex, and should be prepared to act accordingly.

DEPLOYING LANGUAGE AND DESCRIPTION

Good description can add powerfully to any message. There is all the difference in the world between saying that something is "smooth as silk" and describing it as "sort of shiny". Things that are inherently difficult to describe can create a powerful impact if a well thought out description surprises by its eloquence, precision and appropriateness.

This is especially true of anything where the phraseology is not just clear but novel. For example, once when I meet with the sales executive of a hotel arranging a room for a training session he described a chosen layout to me – a U-shape – as "putting everyone in the front row". Well said, that's just what it is (this is not only a good description, but also demonstrates what is important to the other person; in this case me as trainer).

Conversely, beware of bland descriptions that impart minimal meaning. This means no company's product is merely "quite nice", and something that is "user friendly" nowadays fails to differentiate itself from anything else.

- Use gestures: not too wild, you will be sitting alongside someone, but a suitable level of animation may make a difference to how you sound, contributing to a suitable emphasis, for instance.
- Adopt the right tone: in most circumstances you want to be seen as professional (and exactly what that means was investigated earlier) and usually you want to tailor your style to the circumstances, consciously deciding whether to produce a note of respect, a feeling of attention to detail or whatever. Getting this right is what helps create rapport with others.

- Sound yourself: be professional, but be yourself. And certainly avoid adopting a separate, contrived 'meeting voice'; it does not tend to work and is difficult to sustain.

All these are things that can be consciously varied. Some – elements that suggest/confirm your professionalism – for instance, may need experiment, rehearsal and practice; and to be exaggerated for effect. But together they can combine to produce a satisfactory manner. The effect is cumulative, and this works both positively and negatively. It means that any shortfalls begin to add up, eventually diluting the overall power of what is done. Equally, the better you work in all these areas, the more the effects combine to create a satisfactory overall impression and style.

How your voice sounds goes logically with the way you use language, so we turn next to a few points under this heading.

Using language effectively

How language is used makes a difference to exactly how a message is received. The importance of using the right word has already been touched on, but the kind of difference we are talking about can be well demonstrated by changing no more than one word. For example, consider the first sentence after the last heading: how language is used makes a difference to exactly how a message is received. Add one word ... makes a big difference to ... Now let's see what changing that word "big" makes: it is surely a little different to say: .... makes a great difference .... and there are many alternatives, all with varying meaning: real, powerful, considerable, vast, special, large, important. You can doubtless think of more. In context of what I am actually saying here, powerful is a good word. It is not just a question of how you use language, but what you achieve by your use of it.

Often the talk at meetings is almost wholly without adjectives. Yet surely one of the first purposes of language is to be descriptive. Most writing necessitates the need to paint a picture to some degree at least. Contrast the two phrases used as examples a few paragraphs back:

- Smooth as silk;
- Sort of shiny.

The first (used as a slogan by Thai Airways) conjures up a clear and precise picture; or certainly does for anyone who has seen and touched silk. The second might mean almost anything; dead wet fish are sort of shiny, but they are hardly to be compared with the touch of silk. Furthermore, an even more descriptive phrase may be required; what about a phrase I heard on the radio: 'slippery as a freshly buttered ice-rink'. Could anyone think this meant anything other than really, really slippery?

The question of expectation of complexity (and cognitive cost) was mentioned earlier, and to some extent it does not matter whether something is short or long – whatever it is, if it makes things effortlessly clear, it is appreciated. And if it is both descriptive and makes something easier to understand than readers are doubly appreciative. Clear description may need working at, but the effort is worthwhile.

Making it memorable

Description is important, but sometimes we want more than that. We want an element of something being descriptive, and also memorable. This is achieved in two ways: first by something that is descriptive yet unusual; secondly, when it is descriptive and unexpected.

Returning to the venue theme above, the hotel sales executive, mentioned earlier describing, as part of an explanation about room layouts, a U-shape as being one that puts everyone in the front row is surely being descriptive, but it is also memorable because, while clear, it is also an unusual way of expressing it (unusually appropriate, that is). Such phrases work well and are worth searching for.

As an example of the second route to being memorable, I will use a description I once put in a report. In summarising a Perception Survey (researching the views customers and contacts held of a client organisation) I wanted to describe how the majority of people reported. They liked them, were well disposed towards using them, but also found them a little bureaucratic, slow and less efficient and innovative than they would ideally like. I wrote that they were seen as '... being like a comfortable, but threadbare old sofa, when people wanted them to be like a modern, leather executive chair.' This is clearly descriptive, but it gained from being not just unusual, but really not the kind of phrase that is typically used in business writing. I quote this as being memorable because I discovered it rang bells when I presented the report at a meeting and used the phrase there. It was used later by the organisation's own people to describe the changes that the report had highlighted as necessary.

There are occasions where this kind of approach works well, not least in ensuring something about you is expressed along the way. Some phrases and descriptions may draw strength because people would never feel it was quite appropriate to use words like that themselves, yet find they like hearing them.

Adding some emotion

Another aspect you may want, on occasion, to put across is emotion. If you want to seem enthusiastic, interested, surprised – whatever – this must show. A dead, passive style "... the results were not quite as expected, they showed that ..." is not the same as one that characterises what is said with emotion "... you will be surprised by the results, which showed that ..." Both may be appropriate on occasion, but the latter is sometimes used when it could add to the sense and feeling and there might be occasion to strengthen that – the results will amaze.

Consider this. How often when you are searching for the right phrase do you reject something as either not sufficiently formal (or conventional) given that you are in a "business meeting"? Be honest. Many are on the brink of voicing something that will be memorable or which will add power, and then they play safe and opt for something else. It may be adequate, but it fails to impress, is unlikely to be memorable, and may well then represent a lost opportunity.

Next, we look at some things to avoid.

Mistakes to avoid

Some things may act to dilute the power of what you say. They may or may not be technically wrong in a language sense, but they end up reducing your effectiveness and making your objectives less certain to be achieved. For example:

- Blandness: watch out! As has been said this is a regular trap, but the point is worth emphasising here. This can happen not so much because you choose the wrong thing to say, but because you are operating on automatic pilot without thought, or at least much thought, for the detail and make no real conscious choice. What does it mean to say something is:

- Quite good (or bad), or:
- Rather expensive.
- Making very slow progress

What exactly is:

- An attractive promotion? (As opposed to a profit generating one, perhaps.)
- A slight delay? (for a moment or a month?)

All these examples give only a vague impression. Ask yourself exactly what you want to express, and then choose language that does just that.

- "Officespeak": This is another all too common component of some business writing, much of it passed on from one person to another without comment or change. It may confuse little, but adds little either, other than an old fashioned feel. Phrases such as:

- In the event that (if, is surely better).
- Very high speed operation (fast, or state just how fast).
- Conceptualised (thought).

Worse are the, often American, expressions that infect our language yet have very imprecise meanings; they are usually used in the hope of impressing or making something seem more important than it in fact is, surely thinking creatively or not being influenced by the status quo is better than running something up the flagpole or thinking outside the envelope? A phrase or two like this probably does little harm, but some people seem to develop an "officespeak habit" and most of what they say is like this. Avoid such trite approaches, and work to change the habit of any pet phrases you use all too easily, all too often, and inappropriately.

- Language of "fashion": Language is, of course, changing all the time. New words and phrases enter the language almost daily, often from America and also linked to the use of technology. It is worth watching for the life cycle of such words because if you are out of step then they may fail to do the job you want. I see three stages:

i)   When it is too early to use them. When they will either not be understood, or seem silly or even like a failed attempt at appearing trendy.
ii)   When they work well.
iii)   When their use begins to date and sound wrong or inadequate.

Examples may date too, but let me try. When BBC Radio 4 talks about an "upcoming" event, then for some people this is in its early stage and does not sound right at all; forthcoming will suit me well for a while longer. On the other hand, what did we say before we said "mission statement"? This is certainly a term in current use. Most people in business appreciate its meaning and some have made good use of the thinking that goes into producing one. What about a word or phrase that is past its best? To suggest a common one, how about: "user friendly"? When first used it was new, nicely descriptive and quickly began to be useful. Now, with no single gadget on the entire planet not so described by its makers, it has become weak to say the least.

MAKE WHAT YOU SAY CREDIBLE

It is axiomatic that just saying "I say so," is not often likely to carry the day unless you outrank the group in every way. Even then you may get agreement to act, but not an acceptance that something is right. This reminds me again of the extreme: a manager who habitually said: "It's only a suggestion, but do bear in mind who's making it."

You need to add credibility to any case you make by injecting evidence or proof from elsewhere. This can be done in a number of ways, for example by using:

●   Figures and statistics.
●   Concrete examples and past experience (describing a new project as rather like another that you know people felt went well).
●   Something visual or descriptive.

- The results of a test or trial.
- Expert or objective comment from elsewhere (including from outside the organisation).
- Something in writing.
- Research.

You need to think about when you will need to produce and describe your proof, what will serve the purpose, and how best to put it over.

There is more that springs from this about persuasion in Chapter 5.

Before we discuss the further dynamics of meetings (in Chapter 4), there are two more things to consider in order to communicate effectively in, and get what you want out of, meetings.

AND FINALLY ...
So, at the risk of extending this chapter too much let's conclude with a couple more points that also assist you to make the right sort of contribution.

Timing your remarks
Deciding when to speak is worth a moment's thought. There may be no infallible rules but the best route is not simply to pitch in when the first possible moment presents itself. Make a point too early, and it may be forgotten by the end of the meeting; leave it too late, and everyone one has already made up their minds and are busy planning matters after the meeting has concluded, or the end of the meeting arrives before you have a chance to make your point at all. A few guidelines here may help:

- Do not prepare to speak in a way that will fit only at a particular moment. Fate will likely decree that the situation will not be as you imagine; remain flexible.
- Consider your comments not in isolation, but in the context of the other views being, or likely to be, expressed.
- Play to your strengths: are you best at introducing, developing, or summarising an argument?
- Make your future intentions clear. Reserve the right to make a further comment later, addressing the Chair and getting their agreement: "I have some thoughts about costs, too; perhaps I can

come back to that later in the agenda".

The worst mistake is probably to leave things too late. If you perpetually wait for some imagined "best moment", it may never come, and you may end up either not making your point or else making it, by default, at a bad moment.

Finally, how should you approach all of this?

The right attitude

Meetings demand active participation. You have to be on your toes, with your wits about you, ready to contribute in a considered, fine-tuned way as the meeting progresses.

It helps if you:

- Remain alert and concentrate on everything that is going on throughout the process (even if some things are of less interest to you).
- Listen – carefully – to everything that is said and make notes as necessary.
- Observe what other participants are up to, how they are reacting, and make plans in the light of this.
- Keep thinking – and always engage the brain before the mouth whenever you speak.
- Remain calm and collected, whatever the provocation and however far from your anticipated vision of the meeting the actuality strays.

There is a lot to think about here. You have to bear in mind several of the factors commented on in this chapter simultaneously. Individually, they are mostly plain common sense, but orchestrating them is more complex and may need some thought and practice.

Next we shall look at what can produce both greater complications and opportunities – the dynamics and interactions inherent in meetings.

Chapter 4

THE DYNAMICS OF MEETINGS:
clarifying any confusion

If you can't convince them, confuse them.
Harry Truman

Meetings do not only involve people individually. There are dynamics involved in the way a group works. It is said (cynically) that a meeting is a gathering of people who singly can do nothing, but together can decide that nothing can be done. The reverse could be true. Meetings are there to make things happen, and part of what happens does so in a way that cannot be duplicated by one person working on their own. Something positive is created by the interaction of individuals, by debate, consultation, and the sharing of ideas and experience. Or rather it can be; sometimes the interactions create confusion. Both the positive and negative aspects here must be accommodated.

It has already been said that people should come to a meeting open-minded. More than this, it helps if everyone comes with a constructive belief that the meeting can be made to work, can be creative, and is going to come up with solutions or ideas. This means in turn that participants accept that working together can be difficult. They need to work actively to remove those difficulties as a preliminary to a useful meeting and both encourage and use positive group dynamics to make things work well.

In this chapter we shall consider various additional factors, link them to the power of discussion, and see how different approaches influence events. Also, in the last part of this chapter the question of visual aids is addressed; the use of slides (and other things) can certainly influence the dynamics of a meeting, enhance the discussion and influence the outcome.

First, let us consider a couple of group aspects of meetings.

SOCIAL FACTORS

All organisations have a social structure, or rather a number of interlocking social structures. They feed on contact and communications, for which meetings provide one opportunity. Although it is easy to have too many meetings, an organisation that had none would be a very sterile environment.

Meetings must have an objective and stick to it. But it is fruitless to think that other interactions stop just because we are working down an agenda. People want to meet, to exchange information (and gossip) and, more positively, update their knowledge and extend their experience. Team aspects must be superimposed on this general picture. If it is a team meeting, then (all being well) those attending will positively want to get together; but if with more than one team or simply disparate individuals, rivalries may show themselves and get in the way of smooth business.

Some of the negative aspects can be reduced by both the Chairperson and each individual (who can for instance resolve to keep the gossip in check or meet one or two people just before or after the main meeting). But it may also be necessary to accommodate the social side to some extent rather than fight it – better to reduce it substantially and do so amicably than try to stamp it out and upset people. To give an example: I was recently asked to run a course for an organisation starting at 10am, later than is normal. The late start was because the gathering time was 9am: as the Managing Director explained, "They meet up very rarely and the social side is important. If they get it out of their system at the beginning they will work that much harder thereafter". An interesting thought to ponder, and, for the record, it worked.

Motivation

A good meeting can and should be motivational (positive motivation being maintained by many and disparate influences). It is worth thinking about those factors that can be used to increase the motivation of a group as they meet. For example, motivation will be higher if:

- Everyone understands the purpose of the meeting.
- There are no major conflicts between individual and group intentions.
- There are no "passengers".
- There is trust and respect for the Chairperson.
- Team members are loyal to one another.
- There is prior experience of working successfully together.
- There are no destructive politics at work.
- Confidence is felt that the right team has been assembled.
- Hierarchy does not interfere with debate, for example by restricting free comment.

Sometimes there are real contradictions that cannot be avoided; for example, individuals having to come to terms with something that will work for the group but be inconvenient for them. But a well-motivated group will obviously work better than one whose motivation is low. If the factors listed above can be accommodated as much as possible, so much the better.

The right amount of discussion

Throughout this text discussion has been labeled a "good thing", and so it is – up to a point. Too little, and the subject is not properly reviewed; too much, and the meeting goes on interminably with points being made that add little to the sum of points already on the table. It is useful to weigh up just how much discussion is going to be useful, not least to curtail time-wasting. The boxed paragraph that follows sets out some pros and cons.

Discussion checklist

Excessive discussion may mean:
- too many alternatives or too much detail to handle at one time;
- too much emotion;
- more frequent misunderstandings;
- the emergence of opposing sides;
- more time being taken to reach conclusions, or no conclusion being reached;
- digressions on minor issues;
- lack of attention to detail;
- circular arguments;
- drift into a lack of realism;
- repetition;
- boredom;
- undue attention to detail – nitpicking.

Restricted discussion may mean:
- withholding key information;
- overhasty decisions;
- disorganised follow-up action;
- no real commitment to decisions taken;
- decisions not supported or implemented later;
- stalemate (with people digging their heels in, when fuller debate might have reached agreement more easily);
- low morale and lack of enthusiasm;
- fixation with the past.

People

It would be a funny old world, it is said, if we were all the same. But we are not, and one consequence of this is that meetings can suffer from a mismatch of personal styles. The first time to think about this is when you are considering who should come to a meeting, although, to be realistic, what you may see as unfortunate combinations are sometimes inevitable. So here we shall consider practical ways of dealing with difficult people (the solution may lie with the Chair, but others can take action too).

The talkative

There are often show-offs who want attention, but they may also be enthusiasts for certain topics, which is good. They may alternatively be aiming to monopolise the conversation to overpower others' views and so get their own way.

Solution: The first job is to get a word in. Someone must pounce on any pause (even just a breath!) and call a halt to the flow of words, ideally with a positive comment such as a word of thanks. Then move on, selecting a new starting point or throwing the ball to someone else. You can ask the group a general question such as, "What do others think of that point?" or a more specific one such as, "What David has said raises the question of timing; what do other people have to say about that?" The job here is to avoid talkative people wasting others' time, while ensuring that you do get the core of good points they may have to make.

The gusher

This kind of person is worse than the talkative because he or she has more sinister motives, being intent on drowning others out and getting his or her own point over to the exclusion of others.

Solution: The timed agenda and good discipline will help here. Otherwise, it is again necessary to interrupt, perhaps to summarise or to focus on just one thing the gusher has said: "Before you go on, let me see if I understood what you are saying about Stage One. You think…" Control the gusher carefully when they rejoin the debate.

The Sphinx

Silent people also present problems, especially if you know they do have something to contribute. The reasons for their silence may range from shyness to boredom to indifference.

Solution: Asking questions (and waiting for an answer) is the best tactic here. An easy comment may be requested first to get them talking, followed by requests for more details. If someone is holding back for reasons other than those mentioned above, a more direct approach may be necessary: "You have a lot of experience with this, what do you think?" (And, yes, a little flattery may help).

Separate "meeters"

Whispered conversations as the meeting proceeds are distracting for everyone. They may, however, be constructive or negative.

Solution: pausing isolates the chatter and draws attention to it (often this is sufficient to stop it). Then you can identify what is going on, find out whether it is relevant (you may want to digress or flag it as something worth returning to later), or whether it is to be bypassed promptly.

Note: These days the separate conversations that interfere with meetings often consist of electronic communication. The more mobile phones do – text, surf the internet, link to social networking sites and so on – the more the temptation to communicate outside the meeting room seems to be. Many organisations and people habitually in the Chair have rules about this – most obviously "Switch them off" – and I heard a meeting introduced recently with both the injunction to switch off mobile phones and a demand for a contribution to a named charity if anyone's phone rang.

Chip-on-the-shoulder

This is the sort of person who has a pet gripe or who feels hard done by in some way. Whether the grievance is justified or not, do not take the meeting to be the place to pursue something that is surely a separate issue.

Solution: find out whether the gripes, especially unspecific ones, conceal a real point. Ask the person to be specific. Refer back to the purpose of the meeting: "Will this help us to…?" Use the group (and time) to confirm the need to concentrate. Promise – if appropriate – to come back to the sore point on another occasion, but get the conversation back on track.

The devious

There is, let us be honest, sometimes rather a lot of deviousness about. There are also many reasons for people not to say exactly what they really feel or mean. These can range from simple fear of losing face to concern with long-term strategy. What people say may underplay, overstate, or disguise the facts, even to the point of sometimes being, let us say, economical with the truth.

Solution: here the good meeting operator learns to read between the lines. Unless you recognise that something beyond the meeting's objectives and content is going on it is difficult, if not impossible, to deal with. The options here vary widely. Sometimes longer-term issues need to be taken forward in parallel with immediate ones. Sometimes deviousness must simply be stamped on, openly and firmly. This may well link to the question of office politics, which is addressed later.

The aggressive bully

Some people will ride roughshod over everything, including rules and normal behaviour, to achieve their aims. There may be many reasons: desperation overbalancing discretion, perhaps.

Solution: this needs firm action taken without delay (waiting to "see if it gets better," is really not an option) and made to stick. Lay down the rules, lay down the law, and use the group to back you up. Being in the Chair carries responsibility, and may well demand clout on occasions.

The above examples illustrate the complexity of "people issues". Sensitivity to these is always necessary. Sometimes they do not cause great problems; sometimes the solution is found by playing one person off against another (for example, getting a member of the team to "squash" the talkative person) or by pairing people off (sitting a silent person next to someone able and willing to take the time to encourage them); but sometimes – if they are not addressed – these issues can run the meeting into a siding or derail it completely. Although some of the action identified here falls most naturally on whoever is in the Chair, everyone can assist if they take a constructive view and act to help make things go well.

HIDDEN MOTIVES

The office where office politics do not exist does not exist. There are political office environments, very political ones – and not much else. As Sir Ernest Benn said, "Politics is the art of looking for trouble, finding it whether it exists or not, diagnosing it incorrectly, and applying the wrong remedy." Political factors range from those aspects which are potentially able to exert dramatic influences – such as a company unexpectedly bought out by new owners who impose change, including replacing people – to minor matters of personal advantage. While political tactics should not be seen as a magic formula for success with the ruthless politician contriving their way to the top through an unstoppable series of coups (though this does happen), there are undoubtedly those who regard the organisation as a highly political stage – and nowhere does this show itself more than in meetings.

So this is an area to note and there are some principles here that can be treated in just the same way as the other plans you make and tasks you set yourself with an eye on effective operation. First, let me suggest an initial response.

Match yourself to the corporate culture

I mean this in a practical and considered sense, and in two rather different ways that are perhaps best described by an example. First, before I set up my own business, I worked in a medium-sized consultancy firm employing about one hundred people. What made the firm profitable was having sufficient work of the right kind, at the right time and the right fee level. The culture of the firm reflected this fact. Two key ways in which people were judged were:

- Self-sufficiency – producing a volume of work they could do profitably and hitting their own financial targets.
- Selling more work than they could do personally and thus helping fill the work schedules of others less skilful at selling.

Of course, there were other things, not least quality of work. But, though it would sometimes be denied, the two above were most important and someone doing excellent work but not hitting their target, maybe by a small margin, would not be so well regarded. Without a doubt, being self-sufficient and selling more than you could do helped someone get on within the firm. Every organisation has such factors as these and you would do well to think on what they are and what action you should take to get the most from the situation.

Secondly, though perhaps less practically linked to organisational work, there are other more social factors. An organisation may build up a cadre of senior people who all share the same interests or activities. In one firm, this may mean many internal decisions are made on the golf course or in a particular bar after office hours. This may be more difficult to fit in with, and just taking up golf or whatever may not see you instantly welcomed into the inner sanctum anyway, but should be observed and considered.

This is less a question of being what might be called a "company person", than of taking the most practical opportunities offered (the consultancy example above is a good one in this respect); apart from anything else you do not want to be seen to be striving to "fit in" in a contrived way as this is self-defeating in terms of the effect it will have on others.

Assess and know the opposition

Teamwork is essential to any successful enterprise. Yet it is simply not true to imagine that an organisation is one big, happy family with everyone sharing the same feelings and ambitions; indeed, those present around a meeting table may sometimes evidence this fact. All organisations are to one degree or another hierarchical and all are pyramid shaped. There are, as they say, more Indians than Chiefs. Inevitably, therefore, people within an organisation are in competition with each other, not equally for everything of course, but how you progress and are able to operate is influenced, in part at least, by how others, particularly those with similar intentions, conduct themselves.

To be effective therefore you should reflect an active and ongoing appraisal of this fact. Consider: who specially is likely to influence your position and intentions? And how are they likely to proceed with their, possibly incompatible, plans? Honest and open (though there are always unseen undercurrents) competition is to be expected. However, out and out politicking is much less to be recommended, though of course it does happen, and if the knives are out then self-defence has to be the order of the day. Unfortunately, this kind of approach tends to be bad for the organisation, breeding suspicion, lowering motivation and resulting in more time being spent watching backs than on the job in hand. Additionally it can create confusion, which similarly distracts from real tasks and issues and may explain why some meetings unaccountably fail to find accord.

However such things proceed, you should take how office politics works and, in particular, other people into your thinking and act in a way that assesses realistically how it all changes the situation. Sometimes such an assessment will send you off on another track, adapting your intentions perhaps because the cut and thrust is simply too much for you. On other occasions you have to resolve to gear up for fierce competition. But perhaps achieving success would be no fun if it was too easy! At meetings this sometimes means that what initially seems a simple point to put over is, on reflection, more difficult: you anticipate objections and step up your persuasive powers.

Watch for signs of likely change

Horror stories abound of signs of impending doom. In one American company it was said that the signs of your personal position faltering involved the telephone. Occasionally someone would sit down at their desk and find their phone was "dead". On contacting the operator to report the fact (using another phone), a polite voice would inform them that they no longer needed a telephone – unpleasant. Here I mean to commend the simple, practical advice of keeping an ear to the ground and your wits about you, especially before and at meetings.

Sometimes, someone says that they are too busy for politics just before something occurs to their disadvantage; something which they would have seen coming a mile away if they had only looked up. Being busy, for whatever reason – and for many it's the norm – must not blind you to what is going on around you. I once saw some office graffiti saying, 'It is difficult to see the writing on the wall if your back's to it.' It is a fair point.

Of course, we must remain constructive. The reason to watch out is only in part to watch for warning signs; it is also to watch for opportunities. For example, in one company two executives worked closely together and got on well. One day, the more senior of the two confided that he was seeking to work overseas. "In a year or so I will be on the other side of the world," he said. After he duly resigned a meeting was called to see what reorganisation this meant. His colleague was able to present a cogent case to their joint boss's recommending that he took over as the department head, showing why he was well-equipped to do so and how he could rapidly re-staff to fill the gap his move would leave. What is more, he had made sure during that year, when he knew what was likely to occur, that he took some self-development action to make sure he had a good chance of the plan being approved. Is that office politics or sensibly taking advantage of circumstances? Certainly it is a good example of a meeting going well because observation and then preparation preceded it.

Never cut off your options

I think this heading states the most sensible and useful piece of advice I have ever been given in this area. Realistically, the options you have, in whatever you do, are more like a river constantly branching into tributaries than one straight road. There is rarely advantage in rejecting privately, or taking action that rules out, any particular path immediately. Unless you are genuinely clairvoyant (in which case what are you doing reading this? You know what surprises your next meeting may spring!), you never know which will be the best route. Circumstances change. What seemed like a long shot suddenly becomes a real possibility, or what seemed secondary becomes your best option – provided you have not ruled it out. So keep all your options open and only do away with any for good reason (it is possible sacrificing one will open up another, and perhaps a better one, but this should be a conscious decision).

Your approach to all this should have a good deal in common with strategy. You need to take a strategic view and the rule discussed here is in fact just one aspect of this process. At the risk of introducing yet another topic you need to know about, you could do worse than to read a little about strategy and, if you want to give business books a rest for a moment, read James Clavell's novel about Japan: *Shogun*. It has more in it about strategy than most titles with the word in the title (and it is an enthralling read).

Symbols of success

Somebody once coined the term "executive toys" for desk gadgetry of various sorts; primarily for the tacky type such as those things that roll stainless steel balls into holes marked 'yes' and 'no' to aid decision-making. The choice of such things, if any, should be treated with care. Some people go to some pains to cultivate an image in this way, ensuring that they have the right newspapers or magazines around the office, that the clock shows three different time zones, and the wall and bookshelves are stocked with the right kind of pictures, certificates, and business titles to show that the office is occupied by a thrusting and high powered executive.

The trouble is that many of these things can backfire. The clock may not be seen as a symbol of international connections but as pretentious. Someone who has actually read one of the books might ask you about its content and so on. Probably the only reasonable advice is moderation and care. Personally, I would settle for surroundings that are straightforward and businesslike rather than risk something being taken the wrong way. That is not to say that you cannot have a few homely touches, though it is good if even they have some relevance. Amongst other things on my office wall is a print showing an original illustration from Lewis Carroll's famous book *Alice in Wonderland*. The words reproduced alongside the picture of Alice in conversation with the Cheshire Cat run as follows:

"Would you tell me, please, which way I ought to go from here?"
"That depends a good deal on where you want to get to," said the Cat.
"I don't very much care where ..." said Alice.
"Then it doesn't matter which way you go," said the Cat.
"... so long as I get somewhere," Alice added as an explanation.
"Oh, you're sure to do that," said the Cat, "if only you walk long enough."

As a plea for clear objectives this is not a bad motto for a business; or for an individual. Anyway, I like it.

Why am I telling you all this? Because some such things move about with you; the question of looking the part was mentioned earlier. To this you should add thought about meetings and how you appear not just in terms of your personal appearance, but also how this is influenced by what you have with you – everything from papers and files to your laptop and Blackberry (or whatever technology may be current as you read this). A totally professional and appropriate look is to be recommended.

Be a little paranoid

Assessing the opposition was touched on earlier, but a reasonable view of opposition was taken as being those who are, for whatever reason, in competition with you, directly or indirectly. Sometimes, however, and it pays to be very realistic about this, opposition can have an altogether more sinister meaning to it. Remember the saying, "Just because you are paranoid doesn't mean people aren't out to get you," – many a true word is spoken in jest and organisations can sometimes have something about them of the law of the jungle. Some people, only a few one hopes, are destructive for no good reason, or are spiteful or, for whatever reason, are just not on your side and happy to see you fall by the wayside. This may well be the reason behind some of the unexpected hidden motives that appear in meetings.

I do not wish to give the impression that this is a major factor (much less encourage unpleasant in-fighting) but this book would be incomplete if it omitted any reference to the possibility. Advice? You should be, in a word, watchful. Read between the lines, take a little while to form views of people, be especially wary in difficult or changing times – adversity sometimes brings out the worst in people – and treat remarks like "Trust me" with a degree of caution. There may not be an assassin hiding around every corner, but you may well meet one or two ill-intentioned people over the longer term. Forewarned is forearmed.

Overall, what is required here is an awareness of the political nature of the workplace and a resolve to accommodate what this implies into how you conduct yourself before, during and after meetings.

USING VISUAL AIDS

It is hardly necessary to point out the relevance of visual aids to meetings; it is the absence of slides, and particularly of Microsoft's ubiquitous PowerPoint, that is now unusual. So, while visuals are not always either necessary or used, I offer no excuse therefore for focusing on this methodology. But firstly more can be involved than just slides.

First principles

Perhaps the most important visual aid has already been mentioned: you. Numbers of factors beyond your profile and presence, such as simple gestures (for example, a hand pointing), and more dramatic ones like banging a fist on the table, which may be described as flourishes, are part of this, as is your general manner and appearance and one specific factor: whether or not you stand up. The art of formal presentations are another matter; here the norm in the kind of meeting reviewed is people assembled and seated around a table. But standing up is a valid technique and it certainly focuses attention. Perhaps not a technique to overuse, but it has its place and is worth considering.

Beyond the individual, more tangible forms of visual aid are also important. Such items as slides or a handout (passing round a chart or diagram, perhaps) serve several roles, for instance they can:

- Provide an element of repetition (a key to learning and retention).
- Enhance a point, adding explanation and emphasis.
- Visualise something (literally painting a picture).
- Aid retention of a message.
- Help add structure and keep track of a developing, and perhaps complex, message.
- Change pace.
- Focus and direct peoples' attention.
- Add humour.

They also help the speaker, providing reminders to them over and above any notes they have on what comes next.

Be careful. Visual aids should support the message, not lead or take it over. Just because slides exist or are easy to originate does not mean they will be right. You need to start by looking at the message, at what you are trying to do, and see what will help put it over and have an additive effect. They may make a point that is difficult or impossible to describe, in the way a graph or pie chart might make an instant point that would be lost in a mass of figures put over solely verbally. Or you may have a particular reason to use them: to help get a large amount of information over more quickly, perhaps.

The checklist that follows deals, briefly, with the various options, offers general guidance on visuals production, and some tips on using the ubiquitous OHP (overhead projector) and, more likely these days, PowerPoint.

General principles of using visual aids

- Keep the content simple.
- Restrict the amount of information and the number of words:
  - use single words to give structure, headings, or short statements;
  - avoid it looking cluttered or complicated.
- Use a running logo (e.g. the main heading/ topic on each slide)
- Use diagrams, graphs etc. where possible rather than too many figures; and never read figures aloud without visual support.
- Build in variety within the overall theme: for example, with colour or variations of the form of aid used.
- Emphasise the theme and structure: e.g. regularly using a single aid to recap the agenda or objectives.
- Ensure the content of the visual matches the words spoken.
- Make sure content is necessary and relevant.
- Ensure everything is visible, asking yourself: is it clear? Will it work in the room? Does it suit the equipment? (Colours, and the right sized typeface help here.)
- Ensure the layout emphasises the meaning you want (and not some minor detail).
- Pick the right aid for the right purpose.

Using slides

Consider the rationale for having any sort of slide first, and never forget what was said earlier: slides should support what you say and not lead it. I have attended meetings where 80 per cent (more sometimes) of everything that someone said comes straight off the slides. In such circumstances people might be forgiven for wondering why they are there. Maybe they could have sent a memo or e-mail instead.

If slides are to be useful they need to be professional and you should bear in mind in preparing for a meeting that originating them takes a little time. It's worthwhile and a poor slide, at worst one that is unclear or ambiguous, may do more harm than good. Incidentally, never introduce a slide with an apology. I regularly hear people say something like, "I am afraid this is not very clear …" especially if it is not original but something taken from something else (a report perhaps), which is very much not a good way to create slides.

One slide may be useful. A series of slides can change and enhance an otherwise solely spoken input. On the other hand, slides should never distract. There are moments when what you are saying is the most important thing and the focus should be on you and you alone. It follows therefore that even when slides are an important part of your contribution to a meeting they should not be dominating or even seen all the time. Yet how often do people switch on the projector at the beginning of a meeting and simply leave it on, with a slide on screen, until the end? Be honest, do you do it? Think too of how far you get beyond one slide, in terms of topic and talk, before you get to another and bring that up on screen. It is not uncommon for people to talk for ten minutes or more with the slide showing on the screen having ceased to have anything to do with what is being said after the first few moments.

This leads us to an important rule

Never forget: only allow a slide to be seen while it is relevant to and fits with what is being said. Do not allow slides to show for longer than they are needed.

How do you do this? With PowerPoint it's easy (yet with groups I meet on training courses I am amazed how many people do not know this). You press the B key on the computer. B = Blank. The screen goes dark and will return to exactly the same place when you press the same key again to continue.

Making this change alone, rather than having a slide on all the time, will improve many a meeting and allow those elements of what you need to say to shine through and be put over to maximum effect. Try it; not least you will see how it moves peoples' attention. Switch on and eyes, and attention, go to the screen. Switch off and they focus on you; for a while at least. An alternative, if you really must have something on view, is to have a "filler" slide: that's something with few or (preferably) no words, but some element of design and colour that is relevant but not distracting. Several copies of this can be inserted into a set of slides wherever you need a pause in specific visual images and for attention again to be solely on you.

So, let us be clear. PowerPoint is a wonderful thing (and perhaps it should be acknowledged here that there are other similar systems). But it can present hazards. If it is ill-used, or simply used without sufficient thought – the automatic pilot approach – it can and will damage your input; at worst it can render what you say ineffective and risk you failing in whatever intention you had.

Some fundamental rules

It has already been said that you should:

- Never skimp on preparation.
- View slides as supporting a message, rather than leading it.
- Not have slides showing throughout a presentation (use the B key).

Let's add another firm rule at this stage. Never forget: do not read verbatim.

Reading is actually quite difficult (actors who record talking books really earn their money). I discovered this myself recently giving talks to promote my travel book (*A Land Like None You Know* is a light-hearted account of a journey in Burma) during which I read extracts; it is something that takes some getting used to. Gore Vidal, being dismissive of President Eisenhower's speeches, once said he was, "Reading a speech with his usual sense of discovery." But that difficulty apart, reading presents other problems not least because people read to themselves seven times faster than you can read out loud (yes, really, think about it); if you read you will always lag behind and attention will be compromised as people move between reading (to themselves), listening and waiting for you to catch up.

Things get worse as the text gets more verbose and if it becomes best described as gobbledegook. Looking at this kind of slide – and so many have too many words on – creates gaps when people's minds are free to wander, because they believe they are ahead of the speaker and do not need to concentrate; it just guarantees that your purpose is diluted.

There may be brief exceptions, getting a definition or some numerical point absolutely right perhaps, but otherwise remember what Ben Johnson said "... to speak and to speak well are two things." Consider the mega-verbose slide again for a moment. What could one do instead?

Numbers of things are possible, for instance:

- Use an illustration: an image that can be explained in words, yet has an explanatory aspect and forms a visual prompt to memory; something like a flow chart is a good example.
- Highlight key points in a word (or two), though these words could be superimposed on an illustration of some sort, either immediately or by clicking them in as a second stage.

Back to absolute basics: a typical slide looks like this:

```
----------------------------------------------------------------
Heading
----------------------------------------------------------------
Text
```

Essentially, it is in two parts. It may also be backed by a colour or a design. Make sure that:

- The heading is clear and appropriate: once introduced, and noted by the group, it may be able to reduce in size on subsequent slides so as to allow more room for other elements.
- If you use two headings (one might be the overall topic, featured on every slide, the other describing the current item for discussion – for example, Project A and Timing) make their relationship clear.
- You do not let one element overpower others: for example, you might have a logo of some sort on every slide (why? Because it's visual, coloured or there just as a reflex?) and, if you do, it risks distracting.
- The second section, marked Text above (though it might be something else), can take many forms but must always fit with what is above. If a picture or chart needs more space to make it clear, then lose the heading for that slide (or reduce its size markedly).

A simple checklist slide can be enhanced visually by having one word emphasised; it could appear in a different style or appear with three or four versions of it moving or fading onto the overall image. There are, of course, a host of ways available in PowerPoint to emphasise a word or any other element of a slide – certainly too many to list here. Such methodologies are useful, but they should not be overused, or regarded as adding sufficient interest to render making a slide better in other ways redundant.

All this highlights another principle that needs bearing in mind: that a slide does not have to make sense until you say something about it to create the full message. Following this principle will, by definition, lead you away from wordy slides.

Such a slide may hint at something but it does not even need to do that. Sometimes it makes a better point by not being clear without a spoken caption as it were. It is then what is seen and heard together that create impact and explanation; each playing a different part in achieving whatever purpose is in train.

The intention so far has been to make you think both about general, typical prevailing practice, and about what you do currently. For many people what they do with regard to PowerPoint is, for good or ill, a deeply ingrained habit. You need to see the dangers and the limitations of a pedestrian approach. Then you need to recognise and deploy different ways of using this tool, ways that will be beneficial to the effect you aim to have on your audiences.

Too much technology

Do not let the technology carry you away. Not everything it will do is useful – certainly not all on one slide or even in one series of them. Many people have a reflex: when told to attend and take part in a meeting their first act is to switch on the computer and click on PowerPoint. It's easy to do and it is a common error to allow that ease of preparation to increase the amount on a slide beyond the point where it becomes cluttered and difficult to follow. This might also lead you to use too many slides. Similarly, if you are going to use its various features, like the ability to strip in one line and then another to make up a full picture, remember to keep what you do manageable. Details here can be important, for instance colour choice is prodigious but not all are equally suitable for making things clear.

The second danger is simply the increased risk of technological complexity. Sometimes it is a simple error. Recently, I saw an important meeting have to proceed without the planned slides because the projector (resident in one office) could not be connected to the laptop computer (which had been brought from elsewhere) because the leads were incompatible. Sometimes problems may be caused by something buried in the software. Again not long ago, I sat as someone used some twenty or so slides, and each time the slide was changed there was an unplanned delay of three or four seconds. It was felt unwarranted to stop the meeting and risk tinkering with the equipment, but long before finishing everyone in the group found it disproportionately maddening.

Follow all the overall rules and do not forget, as was said earlier, that you do not have to have a slide on all of the time – when you have finished with one, blank out the screen until you are ready for the next.

Whatever you use, remember to:

- Address the other participants and not the visual aid. Looking at the screen too much when slides are used is a common fault, especially if you are at the head of a table and this effectively means looking over your shoulder and away from any eye contact.
- Make sure visuals are visible (do not get in the way yourself).
- Explain them or their purpose as necessary.
- Mention whether or not people will get a paper copy of them.
- Stop them distracting by removing them as soon as you are finished with them.

Beware gremlins

Is this one of Murphy's Laws? Certainly it is an accurate maxim that if something can go wrong it will; and nowhere is this truer than with visual aid equipment.

The moral: check, check and check again. Everything – from the spare OHP bulb (do not even think about using an old machine with only one bulb) to which way up 35mm slides are going to be, even to whether the pens for the flipchart still work – is worth checking. The greatest modern hazards link to computers: battery level, compatibility of leads and so on.

Always double-check anything with which you are unfamiliar, especially if what you do is going to be significantly dependent on it. And remember that while the sophistication of equipment increases all the time, so too do the number of things that can potentially go wrong. The concept of contingency is worth a thought; what do you do if disaster does strike? Sometimes back up is a sensible precaution: for instance having a paper copy of slides to distribute if equipment should fail in any way.

You have been warned.

Anything and everything

Finally, be inventive. Practically anything can act as a visual aid, from another person (carefully briefed to play their part) to an exhibit of some sort. In a business meeting, exhibits may be obvious: products, samples, posters etc, or may be something totally unexpected. Different meetings, topics and people make different things appropriate. Like all the skills involved here, while the basics give you a sound foundation, the process is something that can benefit from a little imagination.

There is a good deal of detail here, albeit mostly common sense; it represents a lot to keep in mind at one time. Practice and building up the right habits help. Overall, the key issues are:

- Preparation in all its manifestations is simply a must.
- Balancing content and manner; it is as much how you say things as what you say that determines the level of impact.
- Take time; you must allow yourself the opportunity to use techniques not simply rush through the content to get down the agenda.
- Visual aids can help (indeed may be expected), but they must support what is said rather than lead.

So, we bear all this in mind, from preparation to conclusion and dealing with awkward participants, and then the meeting is all over and we can all get back to work – can't we?

Not yet. Any consideration of making meetings work has to take a broader view than that. So next we turn to what happens after meetings.

Chapter 5

AFTER MEETINGS:
What not to forget

This manual has been carefully for any errors
(Title page of computer manual)

One feels for whoever was responsible for the computer manual
mentioned above, but we all know the feeling too of when we did not
cheque something sufficiently carefully (sic). So, it is too with action
that may be due to follow on after a meeting. The temptation is to heave
a sigh of relief as a meeting ends and get back to work, but more is
usually necessary, both in terms of checks and actions.

The key thing after a meeting is that the actions decided upon should
be implemented – as intended and on time, so that the meeting will have
been worthwhile. This may involve anything, from a small piece of
information being passed on, to the implementation of a major project.
Whatever it is, however, it may well need prompting.

THE QUESTION OF MINUTES
Are minutes necessary?

This is a question that needs to be asked. There is more than sufficient
paperwork in most organisations without encouraging more, unless it is
truly necessary. So, in some cases the answer will be "No". In others,
some sort of simple written action reminder (or reminders: it may
involve separate notes to different people) will be worthwhile. In yet

others, where a number of items have been reviewed and there needs to be both an action reminder and a record, then minutes should be prepared.

When they are necessary, minute taking should not be a chore. They should not be an excuse to write at length, recording every word spoken and every aside too (though the asides may sometimes be the interesting bit). To keep them practical, minutes or any kind of action-note should relate to three roles, providing:

- A prompt to action, reminding those who have taken on, or been given, tasks that they should do them – and do them on time. This may also facilitate liaison where several people are involved in an overlapping way
- A tangible link to follow-up, to discussions or a further meeting. This can help ensure that points are reported or taken further. At a subsequent meeting such points often appear on the agenda under the item "matters arising".
- A record of what has occurred, and particularly a record of what decisions were made and what action was decided upon. This may merely be a convenience, a reminder if necessary as time goes by, or it may form an important and permanent record of events, although doubtless you already have enough in your filing systems to make it worthwhile considering how much more you keep, and for how long.

The rule for minutes is straightforward: do not have them unless they are necessary, but do not risk inaction for want of a reminder.

Making them useful

Other factors act to make minutes of genuine use; they should be:

- Accurate: this may seem obvious but it is important if arguments are to be prevented in future – so no sloppiness or omissions, especially of key points!
- Objective: the job of whoever prepares these notes is to report what truly happened, not their embellished view of it.
- Succinct: unless they are manageable, the minutes are likely to

remain unread – "brief but encompassing the key points" is the rule.
- Understandable: avoid gobbledegook or, again, the minutes will either remain unread of confuse the issue. It is useful to number things clearly, the 1.1, 1.2 system probably being the most useful.
- Business-like: their key role is to make it clear what action is expected by whom and when.

See the minutes as a document that has a specific and important role, yet needing to earn a reading, and they are more likely to prove useful.

Format and layout

You may want to follow a planned set of headings. Indeed there may be merit in having all such notes standardised around an organisation, making them easier to prepare and read. Such standardisation must reflect the needs of those originating it. However, there may well be certain standard features that are worth a comment:

- Apologies/attendance: it may well be useful to know who was, or was not, present.
- Minutes of the last meeting: these can be important when the meeting is one of a series.
- Matters arising: as necessary.
- Items discussed: here the relevant facts and decisions are reported rather than a blow-by-blow report of the whole discussion. A reporting style is usually best – "it was agreed that…" – as this avoids any tendency to list what might or should have happened.

This can be followed by such additional items as "Any other business" and administrative matters such as the date of a further meeting.

Once the minutes have been prepared, the next question is who should receive a copy. This may necessarily and usefully include a wider circle than which attended the meeting, but remember not to overwhelm people with paper; ecological considerations apart, there is more than enough to read in most organisations without someone constantly boosting the quantity still more.

The format for such notes is also important. Dense text is to be avoided. They should facilitate the way they will be used – as an aide-mémoire at another meeting perhaps, or as a document that will be annotated. The key things that should jump out from the layout are:

- Decisions made;
- Actions to be taken;
- Who is involved;
- The nature of those actions;
- Dates and timing.

The following example makes all this clear, using just three columns:

	ACTION	DATE
It was decided that a plan would be developed to show the timings and stages of the project – to be circulated before the next meeting	P.F. to prepare the necessary plan	To be circulated by 19 August

The process of taking them

Perhaps it is true to say that the briefer minutes are the better, but they must be done right and it is worth having your thoughts clear about how exactly you will do them ahead of the meeting; if you are taking part in the meeting yourself it needs some concentration to maintain your involvement and also keep a running record. The following points clarify what is necessary:

- *A start before the meeting:* many minute-takers reckon that rather than start the job in the meeting with a blank piece of paper, it is better to work on a pre-prepared format, in other words note down what you can before the meeting to give you a template to fill in. Many details – who is expected to attend, timings, agenda etc. – are available ahead of time and doing this certainly makes the on the day job more straightforward.

- *Record all the essentials:* the base information must be right – date, times, names and so on as well as formalities such as recording the approval of previous minutes (where a series of meetings is in train).
- *Attendees:* have the names of those expected to attend (and note for instance how to spell them correctly); note any apologies and also the names of any people who arrive late or must leave early (as they will miss some of the discussion). In some circumstances it may also be useful to pass round an attendance form so that people can sign in (and maybe record other details that may be necessary afterwards, such as email addresses). Another useful device is to draw a "map" of the table and show who is sitting where to make it easier to note quickly who says what.
- *Avoid verbatim reporting:* it is rarely necessary to record everything said. Most often a record of the gist of discussion and specifics such as objections and decisions taken is sufficient.
- *Method:* most often this will just be your own personal "shorthand", though of course some minute-takers will use actual shorthand and certain meetings may be so important that they are recorded.
- *Participate:* as has been said, being the minute-taker means taking extra care over your role as a participant, so be sure you have prepared that and have ready questions you want to ask or points you wish to make.
- *Write soon:* it is good advice to write up your notes as soon as possible after a meeting. However good your note taking, your notes are likely to make less sense to you as time goes by and other matters impose on your thinking; besides, their prompt distribution may be appreciated, indeed may be necessary, in their role as prompts to action that may be urgent (people may wait for their arrival before taking action, so delay can cause problems). Prompt action is equated with efficiency and courtesy and may also make a good impression.
- *Check:* if necessary check what you have written with an attendee (most obviously the Chair) before distributing copies. It is often sensible to get people to acknowledge receipt of minutes, especially if they are distributed by e-mail.

- *Corrections:* remember that when a meeting starts by approving past minutes some changes could be necessary and this too needs to be actioned promptly and a new copy circulated if that is required.

MEETING PROCEDURE

Some meetings are more formal than others. The checklist (about procedure) that follows summarises the essentials and provides a quick review for those whose meetings are light on formalities.

Meetings need to be disciplined, though not so much (as we have seen) as to stifle debate and creativity. Perhaps, therefore, the best rule is that there should be as few rules as necessary, or as the circumstances allow (some meeting are constituted in such a way that more are indeed necessary, as for example with an association).

That said, there certainly are some guidelines that may be worth bearing in mind; draw on these as appropriate to help keep your meetings running smoothly and constructively.

Here are a few general points first. You might wish to specify:

- The length of notice necessary to call a meeting (and also exactly who can initiate it).
- Where and when it is acceptable to hold it (meetings called for a Sunday and scheduled in inaccessible places have been known to be contrived as a means to reduce attendance and voting).
- The form and style of agendas, and also when they should be prepared and circulated; the same applies to the tabling of reports to be considered by the meeting.
- The role of the Chairperson (obeying rules, making comments only through the Chair, for instance) as well as who it is – some committees rotate the role (a sensible idea only if goes to people able to do a competent job).
- Language – for example, no raised voices or swearing.
- That people declare individual interests.

You may think of more issues relevant to your own situation. You may also have to watch out for legal matters (for example, employment legislation in certain kinds of staff meetings).

Greater formality

Where more formality is necessary, there is a number of key factors to consider, any of which might on occasion be important to you.

Quorums

At some meetings the number of people attending is important. If a quorum is required then decisions cannot be made without a specified representative number (of whatever whole) being present. A committee may need, say, 50 per cent present to be able to take matters further. Different percentages may apply to different topics. Routine decisions are no problem, but if we are going to vote to blow the entire budget on a trip to Miami then everyone needs to agree! There are clearly occasions where rules in this area are sensible and can prevent problems.

Motions

This is simply a form of words intended to stand on the record. They are used:

- To start a discussion.
- After a discussion, to summarise and agree action.

Motions may need to be tabled in advance, proposed and seconded formally, dealt with before the meeting moves on, and voted on to make them firm. The way in which this is to work on a particular occasion must be clear to all concerned, preferably in advance. The wording of motions must be done with some care so that it is clear, positive, and unambiguous – saying, "We will reduce the number of meetings held in a year by 20 per cent," is much better than just saying, "Let's try to have less meetings."

Amendments

These add to or subtract from a motion, or change it in some other way. Formal meetings may need amendments, as well as motions, to be proposed and seconded. There are two types of amendment:

- *Constructive*, which add to the case and are acceptable to the view expressed in the original motion, for instance taking the example above, "We will reduce the number of meetings held in a year by 20 per cent and make them last no more than two hours each."

- *Wrecking*, which are designed to change the whole basis of discussion: thus rather than the above the new motion might state "We will *increase* the number of meetings held ..."

Either must be dealt with before the original motion can be adopted or rejected.

Voting

This can take the form of a simple show of hands, or be more complex – and confidential – involving, say, a ballot paper. However it is done, the procedure and the result should be absolutely clear, be recorded, and must not then be the basis for renewed argument.

Points of order/information

These are interjections to the formal proceedings of the meeting, the first used to indicate a breach of agreed rules, the second to correct something that is *factually* incorrect.

Overall, rules should be regarded as a means to an end. They are only to be recommended if they help to ensure objectives are met and the meeting goes smoothly and does its job well. Bureaucracy, after all, can all too easily take over, assuming more importance than the real purpose of the meeting. It was inherent in Parkinson's Law that the man who is denied the opportunity to make important decisions begins to regard as important the decisions he is allowed to take. This is a fitting warning in a review designed to focus, above all, on the constructive role of well-run meetings.

SUMMARY

Good meetings do not just happen. That much at least should be clear if you have read this far. But so should the fact that good meetings are possible, and so are meetings that achieve great things. It is never "just a meeting". Think what you want to achieve, aim high, manage the detail, and all really can go well.

Onto the last item on the agenda

And now, any other business?

Yes: an important point – never end a meeting with the ubiquitous 'AOB (Any Other Business). This can jeopardise even the best-run meeting. As you come towards the end, and everyone is expecting to get away, suddenly the Chairperson is heard to say "… and now just a few items of AOB…" The meeting can then nosedive into a mess of bits and pieces, gripes and irrelevances, and people leave irritated. The impact of a good meeting is lost.

It can work well to *start* with AOB: "Let's take 10 minutes to get a few points out of the way quickly, then we can get down to business." Remember that although AOB items can be requested in advance or on the day, they do not have to be included; too many meetings contain items that are of importance only to a couple of those present, and that would be better dealt with between the two of them on another occasion.

Some meetings are necessarily a routine; others are important and should serve to inject enthusiasm and commitment for courses of action discussed. So, where appropriate, end with a bang and send people away not with the AOB gripes as the last item, but on a high note.

That's it. Well, that's it in terms of sequence, but beyond the interactions described in the chapters so far some meetings and some topics demand more specialist forms of communication: the most common is the need to be persuasive to gain acceptance for your point-of-view and/or to obtain agreement and prompt specific action. The next chapter investigates how to go about this and how to add an element of negotiation when that is also required.

Chapter 6

SPECIAL COMMUNICATION:
Gaining acceptance

Chance favours the prepared mind.
Louis Pasteur

Of the many kinds of communication that are necessary in meetings, whether you run them or just participate in them, two need particular additional skills; they both have to do with getting agreement and are being persuasive and negotiating a deal.

Fact: agreement rarely falls into your lap. You have to actively win it. And you may have to overcome a distaste to do so. After all, the archetypal image of, say, a pushy double glazing salesman, is not an entirely positive one. The good news is that the individual techniques of persuasive communication, which is the general version of selling, are pretty much common sense. They are understandable. They are manageable (at least with practice). You *can* do it successfully. What is more, doing so can engender considerable satisfaction. It is always good to obtain agreement. It is better still when you can look back and say *I made that happen.*

PERSUASION

Because persuasion secures agreement and negotiation agrees the terms of that agreement, it is logical to refer to persuasion first. Any complexity in the specialist techniques of persuasion comes from the fact that there are many different factors in play; and many different techniques. The trick is in their appropriate deployment and co-ordination. Being successful at persuading is dependent on several factors:

- Understanding how the process works, and how the techniques can be used.
- Deploying the appropriate techniques.
- Focusing on the other person rather than solely yourself.
- Communicating clearly.
- Actively directing the interaction.

So, let's consider what is necessary to inject an element of persuasion into your contributions to meetings.

What is persuasion?
It is simply the process of communicating a proposition or idea in a way so that it is agreed and which usually results in a subsequent action. Thus, for example, if you were trying to persuade your boss to give you a salary increase, you would be successful not just when they agree that "you deserve more", but when the first increased pay cheque is in the bank. To be a successful persuader you need to recognise that:

- Your perspective and that of whoever you aim to persuade are different (as when a customer wants good quality or service and the best possible value for money and the seller wants revenue and profit, now!)
- Persuasion acts on someone to influence their decision.
- Your job is to make your case clear, attractive and credible.
- You do so in a competitive environment; for instance, often people are exploring different options for action in parallel – plan A or plan B – and the same principle applies if you want funding approved for a project (the money could be available, but spent differently).
- Part of your job, therefore, is to differentiate from other propositions.
- The process involves selling yourself, in the sense that the other

person must trust you and come to value your opinion.
- How you go about it is as important as what you do.

If you are knowledgeable – about the matter in hand and about the process of persuasion – this gives you confidence. This, is turn, communicates itself outwards – it is read as professionalism. Everything you do is predicated on this fact. Knowledge is power, certainly a lack of knowledge can well inhibit agreement. For example: you know yourself that if you are buying, then any display of poor knowledge about a product rapidly knocks your confidence in everything that is being said to you.

Definition: the following may seem simplistic, but it provides a solid foundation to make everything you do here easier: persuasion is helping people to make decisions. Usually a decision will be made. Your job is to help this process, and – as you do so – to ensure that your own proposition is the one chosen.

The decision making process
Consider. how do you decide to buy something? You review the choice – say a new car – and an initial filtering of possibilities quickly produces a short list. You decide to investigate say a number of five-door hatchbacks.

What next?
You want to know something about them:

- The good points: sensible petrol consumption, aspects of performance, styling and safety features such as ABS brakes. There is a complex list of considerations.
- The less good points: maybe such things as high insurance costs or higher than average depreciation. Again there may be a number of points.
- The organisation: in this case both the manufacturer and the distributor. Are they reliable? What happens if some fault were to appear? Here again there may be a profusion of points good and bad.

Your decision is made having weighed up this balance. You want the case to be good. But you may compromise: selecting the sporty model despite the high insurance, say. You do not expect there to be no snags, though hopefully only what you regard as minor ones. You select the overall package that appeals, that provides value for money and – above all – that meets your needs.

This is exactly what everyone does. Whatever it is you are doing, your job is to help them. Usually a decision will be made, the question is when and how the decision will be made. You can influence both factors.

What this needs is a systematic approach. As we dissect the process, and look at it, stage by stage, remember that this is only to produce familiarity that will ultimately enable you to talk fluently; in a way that will make others feel comfortable.

Preparing to succeed

If there is any sort of magic formula about such particular communication, it is here. Good communicators always do their homework, especially when aiming to persuade. A plan should not be a straight jacket, Because you cannot ensure everything will go as you might like, it must be flexible. It is like a route map. Useful when all is going to plan to keep you on the ideal route. But also useful to help change direction when something unforeseen happens, allowing your destination – your objective – to always be in sight.

So, spend a few minutes (it often need be no more) thinking through:

- What you are aiming at (clear objectives are essential);
- What you will do;
- What sequence you will use to put over your case;
- What emphasis and description you will use to present your case;
- Whether anything is necessary to help the process (visual or other aids: anything that can usefully be shown from samples to graphs or brochures);
- The likely response and questions that could be posed.

With this clearly in mind, you can proceed to the meeting with confidence.

Directing a persuasive exchange
Certain core factors have a disproportionate influence on the likelihood of success.

1.   Getting off to a good start

The initial moments of a meeting are disproportionately important. They set the scene for what is to come. It must be friendly yet professional and businesslike. Indeed, just being organised – in the sense of volunteering a "sub-agenda" (one for your part of the proceedings that shows how you will present your case) – can create the right sort of atmosphere. All you need at this stage is for people to think –"Yes, so far so good, this should be interesting."

Other factors are important at this stage:

* Respect for time: just ascertaining how long someone (usually the Chair) will give you within the meeting and then sticking to time will always impress.
* Creating roles and rapport: the relationship needs setting up. You need to think about how you want to position yourself: as an expert, advisor – whatever.
* Discovering needs: do not settle for superficial information. Prior knowledge – and prior research – is important here. If you do not know enough about how something will be judged and what is important to those doing the judging, ask and ask some more. Make it clear that you need to ask and that your understanding is in their interests. Note the building picture and make sure that, as you proceed, you relate back to it, matching your comments to their requirements. This personalising of your case is vital to being persuasive – and differentiates you from competition (particularly those who have failed to discover as much or to link their case to the facts).
* Linking neatly to making your case: the early stages set the scene and allow you to move smoothly through making your case. Keep describing what you propose to do from the perspective of others, rather than just saying, "I think we should …" Say, "Right, given the facts about timing, in light of the urgency perhaps it would

help for me go through the timescale we would need. I think you'll find we can hit that deadline."

2.   Making a persuasive case

This is the heartland of the matter. You must achieve several intentions as you proceed, and here the overlap with what was said earlier about communication is clear:

- Make what you say clear: this sounds obvious, but often persuasion fails only because someone is left unsure of what they are told; and sometimes a poor case compounds any complexities and make such act as hazards. Think about how you will explain things and make it logical and easy to follow. Avoid jargon. You can score points here as people love it when something they expect to be complicated, turns out to be much easier than expected.
- Make it descriptive: paint a picture and do so with conviction. Your idea or proposition, nor any part of it, must never be "quite nice", or "very practical". Use adjectives. Relate one thing to another. Create a turn of phrase that gets to the core of what you want to put over.
- Make it attractive: the prime method here is through "talking benefits". Sales jargon defines features and benefits as follows:

  – Features are factual statements about something.
  – Benefits are factors that do something for or mean something to someone. To return to the example of buying a car, features abound. ABS brakes, air conditioning, even just the fact of a five-speed gearbox; all are features. The most persuasive case does not just say, "this model has a five-speed gearbox." It links a discovery of a concern for economic motoring (customer's need) with the excellent miles per gallon performance (benefit), the financial saving that this implies (a further, linked, benefit) and tells how the five-speed gearbox (feature) is the reason the model delivers in this respect, thus – "You said how important miles per gallon was to you. You will get excellent economy because this

model has a five-speed gearbox which does an excellent mpg." In other words: benefits lead and create a reason to buy; one that can be tailored to a particular buyer. Features are a source of benefits and begin to make them credible.

- Build up a positive case: point by point you must spell out the advantages – talking benefits, linking matters logically, explaining precisely and succinctly and giving as much detail as necessary to build up a positive balance. While comprehensiveness is never an objective (too often it would take forever), a full picture is, especially one that matches needs. Leaving out a key element of the positive evidence, so to speak, can be dangerous. It dilutes the argument and, at worst, can do so to a level where something else or just ignoring the case seems a better bet. Always remember that a case can be accepted, or not, by a whisker; the details matter.
- Add proof: remember that people may understandably feel you have a vested interest in saying how good something is. Add external evidence – like a motoring magazine's test results on a car's petrol consumption – to reinforce your case.

Overall, the trick at this stage is to remain positive throughout and ensure you present a case that holds together neatly. It must not sound as if you are haphazardly cobbling it together as you go along. It must sound considered and as if trouble is being taken to state matters in a way that is right for the individual(s) you aim to persuade (which, of course, it should be). Referring to things this way will give a more objective feeling, "So, as reliability was so important let's see what we have to offer there ..." and avoid coming over with no more than a "do this" attitude.

People should feel you see the meeting as "working with them", and certainly you should not come over as "doing something to them", putting your own interests first or pressurising unreasonably.

3. Keeping on track

Another job must be done at this point; indeed this may need attention throughout the piece. Remember what was said earlier: that presented with a proposition people literally weigh things up. Use this fact as you explain and people will form a view of what is good and less than good, as it were on a mental balance. You also need to consider the snags.

Some will be raised – "Surely that's not enough time?" Some you should raise (where you know they are unlikely to voice it and it will automatically put a negative in mind if neither party raises it). However snags appear, they must be dealt with effectively.

Your answers do not necessarily have to demolish every objection. They may, after all, have a point. You have to work to adjust the balance. This is not too complicated as there are only four possible courses of action; you can:

- Remove the point from the balance: sometimes an objection is simply wrong; they have made an incorrect assumption or you have not made something clear. The answer then is to put them right, but to do so diplomatically.
- Reduce its significance: here you agree – to an extent – but make clear no great harm is done.
- Turn it into something positive: literally reverse their thinking – "Actually this can be an advantage …"
- Agree it, but put it in perspective: never fight inevitable logic or you will just seem stupid (or desperate). If there is a downside, say so. You can minimise it, and in this – as in all the cases – discuss the point in context of the whole balance and the advantages.

Dealing with objections one at a time, aiming to maintain a positive balance – and not appearing panicked – will keep your overall case positive.

4.　Gaining a commitment

Finally, you need to "close" (as sales jargon calls it); that is to ask for a commitment. Closing does not cause people to agree – everything else you have done does that – but it can prompt action, turning the interest you have generated into action. This action may be to agree – to give something the go-ahead. Or it may be some other positive step along the way – agreeing to a survey or feasibility study, perhaps, ahead of a final decision. Whatever stage you are at needs this positive prompt.

Not closing negates your earlier good work. Checking is no substitute for a close. Ask, "Is that all the information you need at present?" – and you risk them ending matters (at least for the moment) – "Yes, that's been most helpful, let me think on it. I'll put it down to discuss again at next month's meeting."

Closing is not complicated; it may well be no more than a question, but it must take place. You can:

- Just ask – "can we go ahead?".
- Assume agreement and run the conversation on – "Fine, we seem agreed about it all, if you can confirm in writing I'll ..."
- Offer alternatives – "do you want to go ahead with A or B?" (ideally with the first more specifically stated than the second, and with two more to offer if neither finds favour).

You can check out more forms of closing but beware of being too clever; that is, in any case, not usually necessary and can appear pushy.

Finishing off the process

No more may be necessary. If you get agreement, thank them, see to any administrative matters and end matters reasonably promptly (it is possible to ramble on and talk them out of it and no doubt the rest of the agenda stretches ahead).

Or further action may be necessary, for instance:

- Delay: they may say, "I'll think aboutit". Always agree: "It's an important decision, of course you must be sure." But find out why: "... but why particularly is more thought necessary? Is anything still unclear?" This may unearth extra information. For example, that something is unclear (with clarification there and then allowing you to continue, explain and close again), or that the decision needs ratifying elsewhere. Always keep the initiative. Find out when a decision will be reached and volunteer to make contact again so that you keep the initiative and actively prompt the next action. Remember the old saying, 'when people say "We'll let you know." You know,'

Action here may obtain agreement or lead to further stages:

- Be persistent: keep in touch beyond the meeting if necessary. When you follow up take every delay at face value. If someone is out when you telephone (email or whatever), call again. And again and again. It is their timing that matters and you can get agreement by persevering – sometimes after less persistent rivals have given up.

What matters is the success rate. No one wins them all. Some situations demand additional skills being deployed along the way – negotiation (which we get to in a moment), formal presentations or persuasively written proposals. So be it. The job is to do what is necessary. It may not always be as easy or quick as you would like but, if the techniques are well understood and appropriately deployed, you have every chance of being effective. It could be that other related skills, such as formal presentation, are worth investigating if they are relevant and beyond the scope of this book.

Some element of persuasion is often necessary at meetings – it goes with the territory. It is a necessary part of working in most organisations. It will not just happen and few have the qualities of the mythical "born salesman". The secrets of success are understanding the process, planning ahead and making persuasive communication work for you.

Sometimes a natural partner to persuasive communication is negotiation and it is to that that we turn next.

NEGOTIATION
Have I got you where you want me?
Seen on the Internet: advice from Annabel (age six): "If you want a guinea pig, you start by asking for a pony." A force to be reckoned with in a few years time perhaps, she makes a good point; the basic principles of negotiation are straightforward. But deploying them successfully is not so easy.

If persuasion is getting agreement to a course of action, then negotiation goes further: it obtains agreement to the way that agreement will be executed – the terms and conditions that will apply (the "variables" in the jargon). Much of what makes negotiation successful is in the details and in the sensitivity with which the process is approached. Given the dynamic nature of this interactive skill, it is impossible to be comprehensive in what is necessarily a short section (besides there is another of the books in this series, *Negotiation*). So, here we review ten key areas, some of them leading inevitably to others, others linking back to what has been said earlier in the book, which while not together being a panacea, help highlight and summarise something of the nature of the process and the tactics that can make it work. The first is not only important, but also logically comes first.

1.   Be prepared

With a process as complex as negotiation, it is not surprising that preparation is key. Early on it accelerates the value of experience, and beyond that it acts to create a valuable foundation to the actual negotiation that follows. In one sense, preparation is no more than respect for the old premise that it is best to open your mind before you open your mouth. Such preparation must, of course, be combined with that for the whole meeting.

Thus, preparation may consist of a few quiet minutes just before you step into a meeting. Alternatively it may consist of sitting down for a couple of hours with colleagues to clarify intentions and thrash out the best tactics to adopt – or everything in between. It can be stretched to include rehearsal, a meeting to actually run through what you want to happen, rather as you would rehearse an important presentation. So:

- Give preparation adequate time (in a hectic life that also means starting far enough in advance).
- Involve the right people (because they will be involved in the meeting, or just because they can help).
- Assemble and analyse the necessary information (and take key facts to the meeting, for example in negotiations involving money there may be calculations best pre-done).

Preparation should not assume that you can ensure that everything will proceed exactly as planned. Planning is as much to help fine tune what is being done when circumstances do take an unforeseen turn. Experience may reduce the time preparation takes; it does not however make it unnecessary. Remember too the saying attributed to a famous golfer: "The more that I practice my game, the more good luck I seem to have." So, never skimp preparation in terms of time and effort. It is too late when you come out of a meeting that has not gone well saying, "if only I had ..."

2. Communicate clearly

Like preparation, the best way to describe this is as a foundation to success. Your communications – always important – need to be absolutely clear within a complex negotiation situation. There is a power that flows directly from sheer clarity and good description. When people:

- Understand: this speaks for itself, but it also means misunderstandings are avoided and it helps ensure that the meeting stays tightly on its real agenda.
- Are impressed: clarity gives favourable impressions of authority, certainty and confidence – all of which add to the power you bring to the table.

Additionally, clarity about the meeting itself – setting a clear agenda and so on – direct the proceedings and help make it possible for you to take a lead, which in turn helps get you where you want to go.

Clarity stems from preparation, clear thinking and analysis; and from experience. It is worth working at. The last thing you want at the end of the day is to achieve agreement, only to find it retracted later because someone says that "they were not clear what it was they were agreeing to." Insisting at that stage can mean you are never trusted again; it is a position to avoid.

3. Look the part

This has already been flagged as important; certainly it can have a considerable effect on the outcome of negotiating. A sensible view of the literal aspect of this is clearly prudent – you need to be appropriately turned out. More important is that the profile you project gives specific impressions, for instance if you are seen as:

- Well prepared, then people give what you say greater weight;
- Well organised, this has a similar effect;
- confident, this can have a major impact on the credibility of what you say, especially the belief in your insistence that you can do no more if your arm is being twisted;
- Professional, again a whole raft of characteristics may contribute to this from appearing experienced, expert or approachable to something like just appearing not to be rushed; and again the case you make will engender more consideration if the person making it is seen in the right light.

The point here is that something should be done to make any such characteristic more visible where this might help, and sometimes this might become a useful exaggeration. In addition to what is said, many judgements come from visual signals and it is wise therefore to use them.

4. Respect the people

Negotiation is a cut and thrust process. It certainly has an adversarial aspect to it and everyone involved is very much aware of this. While it may be important to take a tough line, to be firm and to insist, this is always more acceptable if the overall tenure of a meeting is kept essentially courteous.

Show that you understand other peoples' point-of-view. Be seen to find out what it is, to note details that are important to them and to refer to this during the meeting. Be prepared to apologise, to flatter, to ask opinions and to show respect (in some cases, perhaps, where you feel it is not deserved!).

Apart from wanting to maintain normal courtesies in what can sometimes be a difficult situation, showing respect can help your case. If you have to take a strong line there is a danger that it can be seen simply as an unreasonable attack; as such the automatic response is a rebuff. If the strong line comes from someone who is clearly expressing respect for others and their views, then it is more likely to be taken seriously, considered and perhaps agreed.

5.   Aim high

This is undoubtedly the most important technique involved. Indeed it conditions much about your whole approach. Aim high. Start by considering, in your planning, what this means. Think about what might be possible, think about what would really be best for you – and go for that. Remember that there is no doubt a list of variables – perhaps a long list – and that what you hope to agree is a mix of them all. Variables are the factors – the terms and conditions as it were – to be negotiated. Essentially, the process here is to trade them on an "if I agree this, will you concede that" basis. Consider what the best position in all areas is – and go for that.

Negotiation is about to and fro argument and about compromise, but it is very easy for compromise to become a foregone conclusion. You can always trade down from an initial stance, but it is very difficult to trade up. Once a meeting is underway and your starting point is on the table, you cannot offer another starting point.

Starting as you mean to go on is an inherent part of aiming high.

6.   Get their shopping list

This rule links to the fact that you need to negotiate a package. If you agree parts of a deal individually, then you reduce your ability to vary the package because more and more of it becomes fixed. Something may seem straightforward in isolation. You are happy to agree it, yet suddenly you come to other points that you want to negotiate, and there is nothing left with which to trade.

The principle here is simple. You need to find out the full list of what the other party needs to agree. Then you must not allow parts, possibly important parts, to be picked off and secured one at a time, as a preliminary to hitting you with major demands at a stage where your options are limited.

7.   Keep searching for variables

Variables can be listed as part of your preparation; listed and prioritised. Even a thorough job at that stage can leave things out. Everything is negotiable, everything is potentially a variable – and this includes things that have specifically been excluded by one party or the other. You may have said something is unchangeable and then decide that you need the additional power that agreeing to shift a little would give you.

Certainly. you need to question what the other party means. Does, "That's it, I definitely cannot go any further on this," mean what it says, or only that someone hopes they will not need to negotiate further about something? Questions, or a challenge, may be necessary to find out. The search for possible variables and different mixes in their respective priority must continue throughout the whole process. As the process demands more compromise from someone then they may have to accept that things they hoped could be regarded as fixed will have to be regarded as variables. And that some variables may need to be more variable than was the original intention.

Keep an open mind, keep searching and assume everything is always a potential variable.

8.   Utilise the techniques

Your success in negotiations is less likely to come from a single clever ploy or one display of power. It comes through the details. There is much to keep in mind during a negotiation, and the situation becomes more complicated as negotiations proceed. You can influence matters in a hundred different ways, but they need to be appropriate ways.

The good negotiator deploys a range of techniques, so they need to be familiar with them and able to make the best use of them. But it is not a question of blasting the other party with a hail of techniques; they need using with surgical precision. Just when is it appropriate to be silent, or to show that you are truly adamant?

Negotiation must never be allowed to take place on "automatic pilot" as it were. Every move must be considered, and this applies as much to how you do things as to what you do. Techniques must be made to work for you and the way to do this is on a case-by-case basis – one that reflects what is right for this person, this meeting and this moment of this meeting.

9.   Manage and control the process

Certainly overall orchestration is a major issue. It is all too easy to find that the concentration that is necessary to deal with the immediate situation can result in your taking your eye off the ball in terms of the total game plan.

You need to take every possible action to help yourself stand back and work with the full picture. For example:

- Make notes.
- Summarise regularly to recap (and always if you feel yourself getting lost; you do not need to say why).
- Keep as much of an eye on the broad picture as on the needs of the moment.
- Keep your objectives and the desired outcome clearly in mind.
- Be prepared to take whatever action is necessary to keep on top of the situation (e.g. to pause and take stock) despite how you think it may look (in fact such action almost always simply increases the level of confidence you project).

If you approach this aspect of the process consciously, note what helps you, and allow positive habits to become established, then your experience and competence will build positively and quickly.

10.   Be forever on your guard

Never relax for a single second. Even when things are going well, when events seem to be following your plan accurately, when one agreement is following another – be wary. Do not relax your attempts to read between the lines in such circumstances and do not assume that the positive path will continue. If you assume anything at all, assume that there is danger, reversal or surprise just round the corner and be ready for it; this is actually a pretty good philosophy whatever kind of meeting you are in.

Remember that both parties are doing their best to meet their own objectives and that the other person is just as likely to be playing a long game as to be a pushover. It is not over until it is over, and it is often late in the day that things come out of the woodwork and change what looked like, until that moment, a straightforward agreement.

Finally under this last heading, remember the words accredited to Lord Hore-Belisha: "When a man tells me he is going to put all his cards on the table, I always look up his sleeve." It is good advice. Similarly when contractual matters are involved, as they usually are in negotiations (and other sorts of meeting for that matter), remember the saying – "The big print giveth, and the fine print taketh away" (J. Fulton Sheen).

By focusing on the ten points above it is not intended to imply the process is simpler than it is, and it should always be remembered that successful negotiation is a matter of getting many details right together. The first step to making it work is to understand the principles and to adopt something of the techniques and how to deploy them. With that in mind you need a conscious approach so that you make your experience build fast, and then note what works well for you, using it to strengthen your future ability to get the deal you want when a meeting demands this element.

Now, about that guinea pig ...

Chapter 7

MEETINGS IN ACTION:
An example

Nobody's perfect, but all of us can be better than we are.
Jackie Stewart

There are so many different kinds of meeting, and not all can be mentioned here, but there is merit in looking at one example in more detail; that of job appraisal meetings. This is not the place for me to commend to organisations the merits of a good appraisal system, one that makes a constructive contribution to maintaining and improving performance standards, though it may be worth noting that in my experience you are likely to encounter different kinds of appraisal in a career that spans a number of different employers and/or bosses. Not all of them will be effective; some managers are bad at conducting such meetings and you may not feel all are constructive. So be it. Careers do not progress in a perfect world, but any appraisal constitutes a major, and potentially performance enhancing, form of communication and you should seek to get the most from them whatever they are like.

That said, appraisal meetings make a good example here first because almost everyone has some experience of them and secondly because the differences on each side – those doing the appraising and those being appraised – are pronounced. It makes the point that:

● Whatever the nature of the meeting it must be prepared and conducted in the light of its unique nature and to achieve its specific objectives.

- Whatever your role in a meeting it must be understood, appreciated and you must reflect that in the way you conduct yourself.

In addition, there are some issues raised here of general relevance to many circumstances, for instance that of dealing with criticism, which can surely come up in many contexts.

THE RATIONALE

Essentially appraisal is simply an approach to improving personal performance in a changing world. Yet, they are too often regarded as a chore rather than an opportunity. Appraisal meetings must be constructive and useful, and can play a significant part in ensuring the good performance in the future that will see corporate goals achieved. So, consider their purpose. Appraisal should act to:

- Review individuals' past performance.
- Plan future work, work emphasis and overall role.
- Set specific goals at an individual level.
- Agree and thus create individual ownership for such goals, making them more likely to be achieved.
- Provide appropriate on-the-spot coaching.
- Prompt action in training and development (and the identification of what may be useful) and thus maintain, enhance and add to skills.
- Obtain feedback.
- Reinforce and strengthen working relationships.
- Act as a catalyst to delegation.
- Highlight long-term career intentions.
- Heighten motivation and commitment.

These intentions are not mutually exclusive, though the emphasis in an individual appraisal may be more on some than others.

Overall, the intention is for such meetings to act as a catalyst to making future performance better than – or simply different from – that of the past. This may sometimes involve identifying and correcting personal weaknesses, but – just as likely – environmental changes, or an organisation's intentions, make changes to what and how things are done necessary. Appraisal must not be a witch-hunt; the focus should always be positive and on the future.

GETTING THE MOST FROM JOB APPRAISALS
It is important to both parties that appraisal meetings are well handled, indeed, as we will see, both parties play their part. For the individual, the key issues here are fourfold:

1. Appraisals: preparing for them

Be sure you understand how the appraisal system in your organisation works before you find yourself in such a meeting. Incidentally, this is a good topic to investigate when you are being interviewed for a job, but before your first meeting you are likely to need more detailed information than is spelt out at that stage. First time round, ask for information if this is not provided and ask some of your longer serving peers how their meetings go, how long they last and what they get from them. Particularly, be sure you know why appraisals are done, how management conducting them views them, what they look to get from them, and what time span the review covers (a year or whatever it may be).

Then you can consider how you want the meeting to go and how you can influence it. For instance, ask yourself what:

- You want to raise and discuss;
- is likely to be raised (and responses to any negative areas that may come up);
- Rating scales are involved (whatever they are you must be familiar with them);
- The link is between appraisal and development and training, and what you hope to get in this area;
- The link is between the meeting and your future work, responsibilities and projects undertaken;
- Questions you want to ask.

If it is not your first appraisal, check what was said at, and documented, after the last one. This must be done in the context of what you now know about the forthcoming appraisal meeting. A couple of points are worth careful planning:

- One is the link to salary review and other benefits. Many organisations separate discussion of this from appraisal meetings (indeed there is a strong case for doing so). If this is so, this cannot be raised, except perhaps in general terms. If it will be discussed, you may have things to prepare here also.
- Another key point is the make up of the discussion in terms of time scale. A good appraisal will always spend more time on the future than on the past, both aspects need thought and certainly there is no excuse for your not having the facts at your fingertips about anything that is a likely candidate for discussion in the review of past events.

Make notes as you plan and take them with you to the meeting – there is no point in trusting to memory and, in any case, being seen to have thought seriously about the meeting will benefit you. You may only get one, sometimes two, such opportunities in any single year. Therefore, some careful preparation will prevent the occasion being wasted, indeed on the overall scale of meetings, appraisals are "preparation heavy".

2.   Appraisals: attending them

The person who is conducting the appraisal will have a bearing on both how it is done and how you need to conduct yourself. If it is with a manager with whom you are on good terms and see every day, this will make for a less formal meeting than if it is someone more senior with whom you only have occasional contact (a number of appraisals involve three people, or more, including the person to be appraised).

A good appraisal will:

- Be notified well in advance.
- Have clear agenda.
- Have a particular duration in mind.

And so these are things you should ask for if necessary. Particularly you may want to have ideas about how much time will be spent discussing last year and next, how interactive the meeting is and when you can ask questions; perhaps also what is, and is not, on the record. Some appraisals are rather checklist in style: the appraiser leads the conversation and raises the points one at a time, asking for your view or comment. Others are more open and allow the person being appraised to lead, pulling them back to an agenda only if the meeting digresses too much. Ideally, you will know which way it runs but you must be ready for either. Remember lack of comment may be read as lack of awareness, knowledge or as indecisiveness. On the other hand, if the question posed needs some thought then it is better to let the appraiser know rather than answering with a hasty comment.

Appraisal meetings should not be traumatic occasions. If they are constructive – and prompting change in the future is the only real reason for doing them – then you can take a reasonably relaxed view of them (provided you have done some preparation) and there is no reason why you should not enjoy as well as find them useful. You are on show, career planning decisions are being made, albeit long-term, by those conducting these meetings, but it is also a positive opportunity for you to present something of your competence in a way that goes "on the record".

3.   Appraisals: the follow up

Appraisals are too important to just file away in your mind or forget about once they are past. They can provide a catalyst to an ongoing dialogue during the year. In many organisations, the system demands that the appraiser documents proceedings, and usually that the appraisee confirms that this documentation is a true record of the salient issues.

But there is no reason why you cannot take the initiative on particular matters. Consider the following as an example. Development requirements are one topic that most appraisals review. This may result in specific action –" I will enrol you on that communication course next month" – or it may result in further discussion, more than can be accommodated in the appraisal meeting itself. It may be useful to volunteer to undertake the processes involved (remember your boss could have a dozen appraisals in the same week and much attendant administration). If you put in a paper setting out some suggestions for action, and if this is used as the agenda for another meeting about it, then this could well see more of what you plan to happen happening – and happening sooner than would otherwise be the case. Similarly, use the opportunity to report back after any agreed training, in writing or at a meeting, so that the dialogue continues. If the training has been agreed as successful then there is logic in discussing "what's next".

A final point – you may think attending them is a chore, but appraisals are not easy to conduct, take time to prepare and always seem to be scheduled during busy periods. So, if it has been useful, express thanks and, if it has not, try to comment in a way that may set the scene for a more productive encounter next time.

4.   Accept and learn from criticism

A good appraisal is likely to be a good meeting. Even if it is poorly conducted and not really very constructive, it is a satisfying feeling to come out saying to yourself "I did well," particularly when someone else has told you so. But unless you believe the graffiti, which says "I used to be great, but now I am absolutely perfect", few of us get through many such meetings without having to take some criticism. We must consider the possibility that it is fair comment. You are probably not perfect, you do not get everything right, excel in all you do and you sometimes get things wrong.

Because, perhaps understandably, no one likes having their failures, even minor ones, aired in public. There is a danger that you simply put such comment out of your mind and concentrate on the good things that are said (almost all such meetings will touch on both). Careers are not enhanced either by repeating mistakes or ignoring failings or weaknesses. If you do not take action after an appraisal and promptly, at least in terms of planning such action, then the moment will pass. Resolve to take note and, if necessary, action and you will do yourself and your career a favour.

Perhaps all this should go without saying, but it is easy to find yourself regarding an appraisal as a rather traumatic occasion, at least to some extent, and forgetting to handle things thoroughly. There is no rule about the order here. Sometimes you will be asked questions or be on the receiving end of comments to which you must respond. But you may need to respond to such with a question – indeed there is often no reason why a question cannot be answered by a question – and there will be occasions during the meeting when you should lead in this way. The alternative is to find you are off target and not talking about what is really required.

Questions can easily be ambiguous (this is possible whoever puts them). This is something that leads us back to preparation. Part of the time before the meeting may usefully be spent not only thinking of what you might ask, but how you can put it clearly and succinctly. Some thought here is well worthwhile, as confusion can annoy and waste time.

Making comments

Appraisals demand you comment on your work and performance. This is what your preparation should have addressed. Your objectives are perhaps to maximise the impressiveness of what you describe and minimise anything negative. You may receive some criticism – more of this later.

The key issues are again common sense:

- Be clear: follow all the rules of good communication; do not go round the houses, beware of inappropriate jargon and get your point across succinctly. This may seem the simplest part of the proceedings, but it is worth some thought. Remember you probably know a good deal more about the details of your job than the appraiser. Remember too that clarity, especially where complexity is expected, impresses.

- Be descriptive: is it sufficient to say you "made a plan", or better to say what kind of plan it was – practical, excellent, creative (cunning? – maybe not). And if it is a creative plan, maybe you should explain – describe – how. Use some well-chosen adjectives to support what you say. There is no reason why you cannot use some visual aids if they would help. Do not struggle to describe complex figures, for example, if one glance at a pie chart would allow the appraiser to see the point in a moment

- Concentrate on implications and results: do not just comment on what happened or was done; rather describe how it was done and especially what came from it. For instance, say for example you saw to the production of a new corporate brochure. You can just mention this, or you can mention how it was produced, your copy writing skills, the deadline being hit or bettered, the way checking out several printers saved money, and the positive reaction expressed by customers about it – or even the business that has already resulted from it. All the later points can be chosen to link in with your agenda and objectives and how you want to put things over

- Provide proof: where necessary, do not just say what happened but demonstrate it, documenting evidence or quoting figures where appropriate. Incidentally, figures which may often be used in evidence must always be quoted appropriately (no 'about 10.26' for instance).

Dealing with criticism

Badly conducted appraisals will often focus almost exclusively on the things that have gone less than perfectly. At worst, the conversation then deteriorates into an argument and as things are banged to and fro nothing very much is achieved.

But any appraisal is going to spend time on difficulties – it goes with the territory so to speak – and you must be ready to deal with this (and the need to do so can crop up in many different kinds of meeting). Three intentions should be uppermost in your mind in this respect, over and above a general desire to put the best complexion on everything:

- Achieving accuracy: here your intention is to ensure that the right facts are considered. Beware of the appraiser using vague statements like "You're never on time with anything". This is unlikely to be true. But what are you late with and what are the implications? It is easier to discuss specifics and questions may well be the route to identify them. Never argue with anything but the true facts, checking what is really meant is the first step to responding to what is said in the right way.

● Giving an impression of objectivity: if every criticism is seen simply to put you into automatic defensive mode, then discussion will be unlikely to be constructive. Using an acknowledgement to position what follows is always useful. It:

    – Indicates you feel there is a point to discuss (if you do not, then we are back to achieving accuracy – see above).
    – Shows that you are not going to argue unconstructively.
    – Makes it clear that you intend to respond in a serious and considered fashion.
    – Gives you a moment to think (which may be very useful!) and sets up the subsequent discussion so that you can handle it better.

Just a few words may be all that is necessary here. Starting with a "yes" gives it power – "Yes, there was a problem with that" – and sounds right even if your intention is to go on to minimise the problem.

Dealing with the points raised: now the job is to deal with the matter. Mechanistically the options are few and therefore manageable. You may need to explain why a difficulty occurred, then there are four routes to handling things (the same approaches that were reviewed in Chapter 4 and are restated here to complete the picture):

1. Remove the difficulty: if possible, you can explain that what seemed like a difficulty or error was not in fact that. A delay, say, might not have been in an original plan, but caused little problem.
2. Reduce the difficulty: maybe you have to acknowledge that there was some difficulty, but explain that it was of little significance
3. Turn the difficulty into a plus: sometimes it is possible to argue that what might initially seem like a problem is in fact not. A delay might not have been in an original plan, but included for a positive reason – there might only have been a real problem without the delay.
4. Agree the difficulty: after all, there is no point in trying to argue that black is white. Most ordinary mortals have some problems during a whole year of activity. Your job is not to persuade the appraiser that there were no problems, but to persuade the appraiser that, on balance, your year was a good one.

THE OTHER SIDE OF THE COIN

What about whoever does the appraising (sometimes more than one person)?

The foundation to success

Successful appraisals need preparation – for both parties: the appraiser and the appraisee. The appraisal meeting needs a considered agenda (which must relate carefully to timing) and while the appraiser has prime responsibility, the appraisee should share responsibility for preparing this. Just "playing it by ear" is dangerous, and risks losing precision.

The appraiser also needs to think ahead. They should be familiar with the appraisal process overall so preparation is primarily a matter of focusing on a particular individual. The appraiser should usually be responsible for directing the process and the meeting. Because appraisal is the culmination of a larger process, a meeting cannot be conducted in the absence of the manager having monitored activity during the year (most appraisals are annual though can be more frequent). At the very least an agenda, timings and so on must be set out in advance.

Then the meeting should go smoothly, though this can only occur if the attitude of those involved is positive and constructive, and this will tend to relate to the prevailing overall organisational culture.

Setting up and running the right kind of meeting

The meeting itself needs some care. Appraisers should bear in mind that:

- The meeting and the agenda should be set up well in advance (and any necessary documentation read ahead of the meeting).
- Adequate time must be allowed – often 90 minutes to 3 hours (results potentially making this time well spent).
- Surroundings must be comfortable and interruptions must be prevented.
- All those involved must agree about the format and the practicality of the proceedings.
- Documentation and any element of "scoring" must be clear in advance.

- Targets and other objectives relevant to the period under review must be to hand, every aspect of the appraisal must deal with facts (not judgements made on hearsay or uncertain memory).
- Discussion must be open, judgements objective and everyone open minded.
- Everybody involved should recognise that listening is as important as talking.
- Sensitive issues must be tackled; peer embarrassment must not sideline them (criticism is part of appraisal, though it must be constructively given and received and lead to change if necessary).

Additionally, two overriding principles are paramount. In a successful appraisal:

- The appraisee does most of the talking (though the appraiser may chair the meeting).
- The focus, and weight of time and discussion, is on the future more than the past (the two go together, of course, but the end results are action for the future).

A clear agenda is thus vital. Stick to it, and avoid digressions. If new topics or opportunities for creative discussion appear, schedule a further meeting and do not upset appraisees by letting time pressures squeeze listed topics they regard as important off the agenda.

The basis for success
Even this snapshot of a specific situation shows how a meeting must work in practice. In appraisal, a poor meeting is clearly a lost opportunity, if not a waste of time. Any meeting must take place in a way that is planned and executed to move purposefully towards clearly defined objectives. With appraisal the whole point is to look ahead, to take action designed to increase the likelihood of future performance being on target and better than it would be had the appraisal not taken place. The details set out here as important to appraisal meetings have their counterpoint in every other sort of meeting; all need approaching individually in terms of the factors that are important to them.

Similarly with any meeting: surely the most important thing is that something changes as a result of it; something moves forward, is improved and the future is more likely to deliver what we want. There is a great deal hanging on meetings; in fact there should be a great deal hanging on meetings (if not, why have them?). The trick is to recognise this fact and make them work.

AFTERWORD

**It is not things in themselves that trouble us,
but our opinions of things.**
Epictetus

The intention throughout this book has been to stimulate thinking in a way that helps make your next meeting more interesting, more constructive, and more likely to achieve its objectives.

Too often meetings are taken for granted. They often appear to be a chore (if they really are, don't schedule or attend them). Additionally our expectations of them are sometimes too low, past experience, too often of poor and unconstructive meetings, influences us in a way that becomes a self-fulfilling prophesy. We experience little and thus expect little, a point well encapsulated in the quotation from a Greek philosopher at the top of this page.

But meetings are, or can be, important. They deserve some thought and your participation in them, whether you are the Chair or not, needs to be made on a considered basis; one that uses appropriate approaches and deploys appropriate techniques in a way that makes you more likely to achieve your aims. Aim high in fact and you might be surprised just how much can be achieved through them.

Running or participating in meetings in an effective manner is not just essential to many jobs and roles and to planning, solving problems, making decisions, sparking ideas and more; it is also a career skill, one that can set you apart, allow you to perform well, even excel, and thus act as a positive influence on how your career progresses. In a word, having and using the abilities described here is an ... opportunity. To redirect a phrase I first heard applied (accurately) to presentations, a meeting is the organisational equivalent of an open goal. It is an opportunity to be taken advantage of carefully, wisely – and, no doubt in most organisations, regularly. Make meetings work and the dividends can be considerable.

Now, I bet you do not have long to wait – what are the objectives for your next meeting?

Patrick Forsyth

Patrick Forsyth began his career in publishing and has run Touchstone Training & Consultancy since 1990; this specialises in the improvement of marketing, management and communications skills. He is an experienced conference speaker and writes extensively on business matters. He is the author of many successful books on aspects of business, management and careers, including *How to Write Reports and Proposals (Kogan Page) and Marketing: A Guide to the Fundamentals (The Economist)*.

One reviewer says of his work: 'Patrick has a lucid and elegant style of writing which allows him to present information in a way that is organised, focussed and easy to apply.'

Other Books in Smart Skills Series

Working with Others

Negotiation

Presentations

Persuasion

Mastering the Numbers

www.legendpress.co.uk